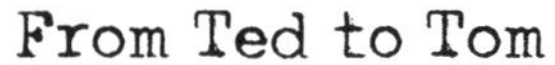

From Ted to Tom

THIS IS A NEW YORK REVIEW BOOK
PUBLISHED BY THE NEW YORK REVIEW OF BOOKS
207 East 32nd Street, New York, NY 10016
www.nyrb.com

Cover design by Jason Booher.

Library of Congress Cataloging-in-Publication Data
Names: Gorey, Edward, 1925-2000, author, illustrator. | Fitzharris, Tom, editor.
Title: From Ted to Tom: the illustrated envelopes of Edward Gorey/by Edward Gorey; edited by Tom Fitzharris.
Description: New York: New York Review Books, [2024]
Identifiers: LCCN 2024015079 | ISBN 9781681379050 (hardcover)
Subjects: LCSH: Gorey, Edward, 1925-2000—Correspondence. | Artists—United States—Correspondence. | Fitzharris, Tom—Correspondence. | Envelopes (Stationery)—Miscellanea.
Classification: LCC PS3557.O753 Z48 2024 | DDC 811/.54—dc23/eng/20240624
LC record available at https://lccn.loc.gov/2024015079

The authorized representative in the EU for product safety and compliance is eucomply OÜ, Pärnu mnt 139b-14, 11317 Tallinn, Estonia, hello@eucompliancepartner.com, +33 757690241.

ISBN 978-1-68137-9050

Printed in Italy.
10 9 8 7 6 5 4 3 2

From Ted to Tom

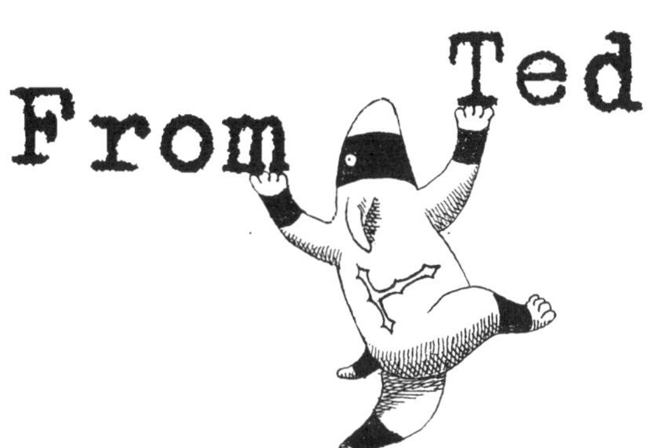

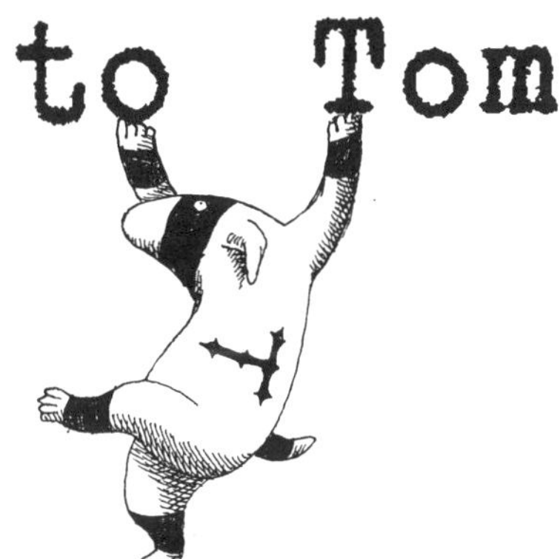

The Illustrated Envelopes of Edward Gorey

Introduction by Tom Fitzharris

New York Review Books

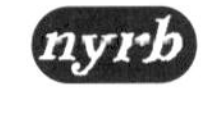

New York

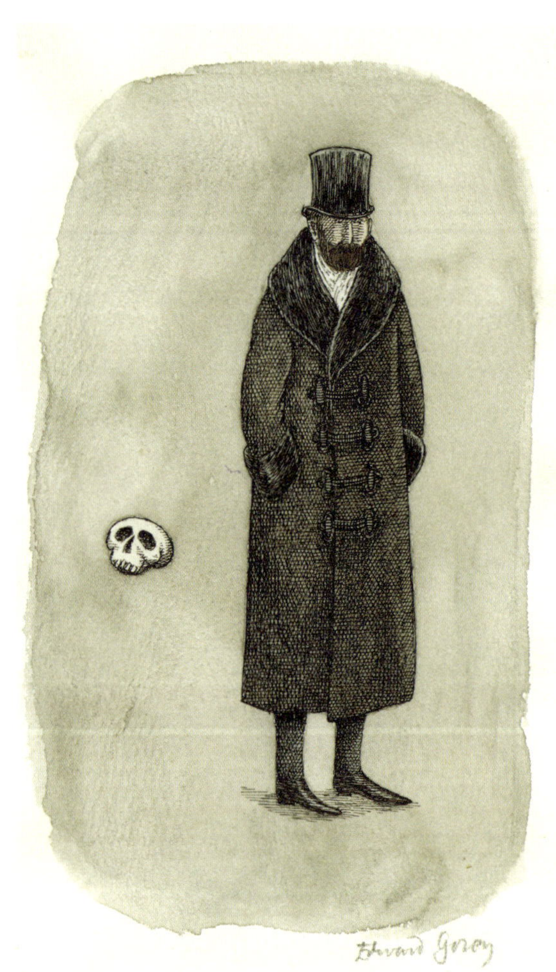
Edward Gorey

Introduction

Before I ever met Edward Gorey, I received a handwritten note from him. In April 1974, he had a show at the Graham Gallery on Madison Avenue. For years, I'd been collecting his small, exquisite books, so I went to the show as soon as it opened. There was a watercolor of a bearded man in a fur coat and Edwardian dress—possibly a self-portrait. I bought it, and asked one of the gallery employees if Gorey would sign a book for me. "Absolutely," they said. "He's a very nice person."

Inside my copy of Gorey's *The Other Statue*, I put in a note that asked: "Why does Victoria Scone bear such an alarming resemblance to the suspicious Miss Underfold?" When I returned to the gallery, Gorey had signed the book and written at the bottom of my note: "Because they are one and the same person."

One afternoon soon after I picked up the signed book, I was walking past Town Hall in Midtown. Gorey was standing outside, instantly recognizable in his fur coat, long beard, and sneakers.

I introduced myself and thanked him for signing my book. I asked him about the nineteenth century French humorist Alphonse Allais, whose "Story for Sara" he had translated and illustrated. Did he know of any other English translations of Allais's work? No, but if I could read basic French, he'd be happy to lend me one of his volumes. (Gorey had his complete works in French.)

It took a while to get in touch through his phone answering service, but we finally met a second time at his tiny apartment during my lunch hour. I had just started my first full-time job, as a photo researcher at a publishing house uptown. I thought I'd be at Gorey's for ten minutes, but I left two hours later. We learned we had dozens of interests in common, including but not limited to dance, movies, photography, art, and stamps. I was surprised I still had a job when I got back to the office. This was the beginning of our friendship.

Ted (as his friends called him) and I began meeting for dinner, the theater, coffee, and especially the ballet, his great passion. He stayed in the city during fall, winter, and spring to match the New York City Ballet's schedule. In the summer, he left for Cape Cod. It was during this time that he began sending me letters.

Ted didn't tell me he was going to do this. The day the first one arrived, illustrated with two dogs wearing sweaters on a house, I called him up to express my thanks. He said, "There will be more." Over the next year and a half, forty-nine more would arrive. After I accidentally tore envelope number one while struggling to open it (you'll see the damage a few pages from now), I learned to be careful, and to always slice the letters open from the side.

It was a surprise each time a new envelope arrived. When the fourth came, I noticed it was numbered. The subjects drawn on them came from all corners of our friendship: details from our conversations, trips we'd taken together, things Ted had seen in junk shops, and often from somewhere within his impossibly wide imagination. As he joked in one letter: "We truly creative people never know what is coming next."

The contents of the envelopes varied substantially. Often there would be a letter updating me on what was new with him: spending time with family and friends in Cape Cod; going to see B movies at the local movie theater, like *Class of '44* and *One of Our Dinosaurs Is Missing*; summer trips to Saratoga to see the New York City Ballet; dance-world gossip; and his musings on what he was reading (often Proust). But mostly he'd be working at his desk in his attic and fending off his cats. I knew two—Agrippina and Kanzuke—but other friends say he might have had as many as five or six.

Ted loved quotations and would often include one (or two) in his letters or inside the envelopes. Lines from Paul Gauguin, Nathaniel Hawthorne, John Cage, and even *The Duchess of Malfi* all made appearances. They were all written in his distinctive, gorgeous hand-lettering on heavy-stock note cards.

There were sometimes mysterious odds and ends in the envelopes too: a nineteenth century pew ticket from a church, funny clippings from the Cape Cod newspapers, even a small piece of a decrepit Toulouse-Lautrec poster with the artist's distinctive logo.

As I got to know Ted, it became clear that he was the best-read person I had ever met. He seemed to have read every work of English literature written in the nineteenth century. He could remember the plots and characters of every mystery novel he'd read, no matter how mundane. His taste in movies and books ran high and low, narrow and wide. Once, looking at my bookshelves and seeing nothing but literature, art, photography, and cookbooks, he chided me: "Where's your junk?"

He would often mark his own books with the days he had bought and finished them (sometimes these would be the same date). He constantly took notes on everything in them: footnotes, parenthetical remarks, and addenda.

In spite of his output of posters, illustrations, stage sets, postcards, and his own books, he told me he thought of himself as a writer more so than an illustrator, and he kept many notebooks. He always had one nearby, typically in one of his many deep coat pockets. He used these notebooks to jot down ideas, grocery lists, or even quick drawings. One contained detailed sketches of every envelope he sent me; when two envelopes he sent got lost in the mail, he was able to redraw them exactly.

During our friendship, Ted and I visited Scotland. It was one of the only trips he ever took outside of the United States. I'd been there after my service in Belgium was finished; and when I decided to go back, I invited Ted. We traveled the countryside for a few weeks before returning to New York together. The intensity of our correspondence inevitably ebbed. At some point, I just stopped hearing from Ted. A little while later, I got a letter saying that one can't predict when things will end or how they'll run their course. It was unsigned, but I knew it was from him. Over the years I'd bump into him at plays and movies. He was always funny, always cordial. When I traveled, I'd send him postcards, but I never heard back. When he moved permanently to Cape Cod, I never saw him again.

He was modest, often cryptic and indirect, but despite his frequently somber artwork, he was not at all gloomy in person. Some gallows humor? Sure. Exaggerated, dire warnings of impending doom? Yes. But gloomy? Never. Ted was incredibly playful and loved to laugh, often at himself. When I think back on that time with Ted, that's how I remember him: laughing.

These envelopes are only a sliver of our friendship and of his work but remain full of his life and special wit. As he put it himself in one of his letters: "Even a haiku can make you feel that everything was somehow included in it."

—Tom Fitzharris

A Note from the Editor

The following pages present all fifty envelopes that Ted sent me from 1974 to 1975, along with excerpts from his letters, note cards, and other items he slipped into his envelopes. At the back of the book, there is a section of notes where I talk more about the references for the quotes, the inside jokes of the letters, and the details of the drawings.

We hold these Truths...
UNITED STATES 10c
JUL 8
1974
TOM FITZHARRIS,
39 Hickory Hill Road,
Eastchester, N.Y.
10709

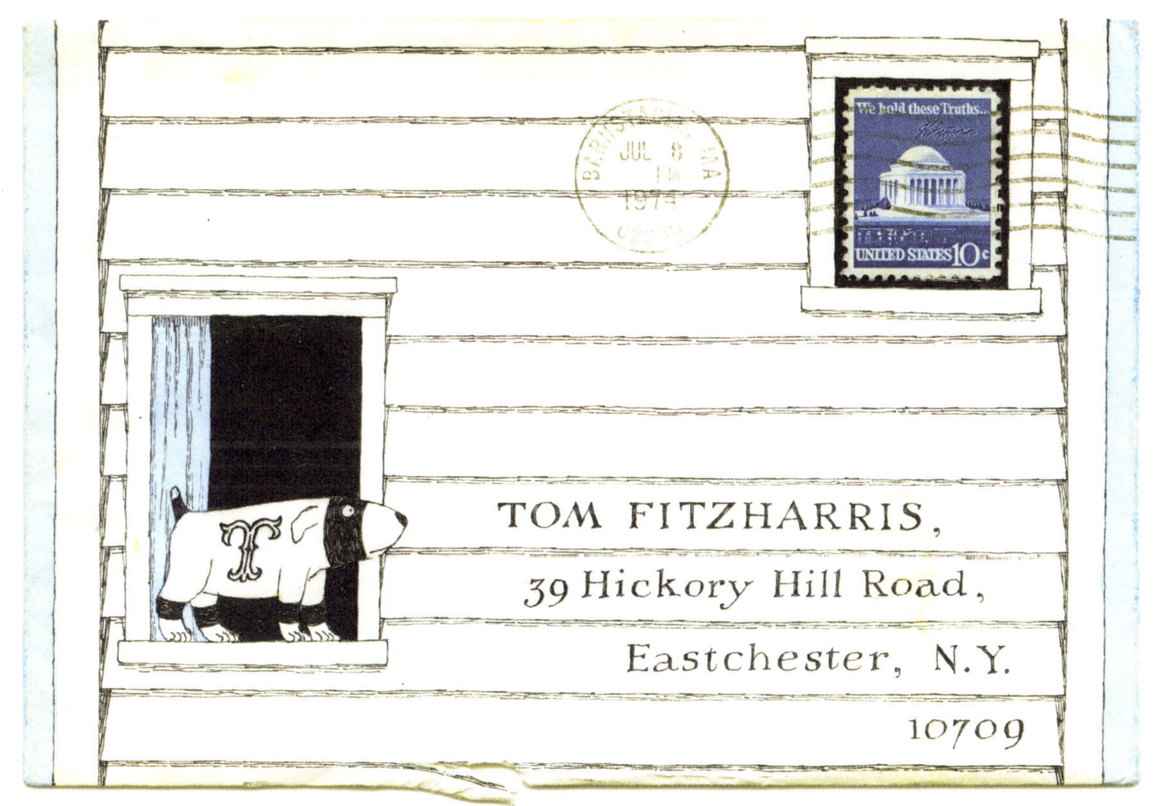

One

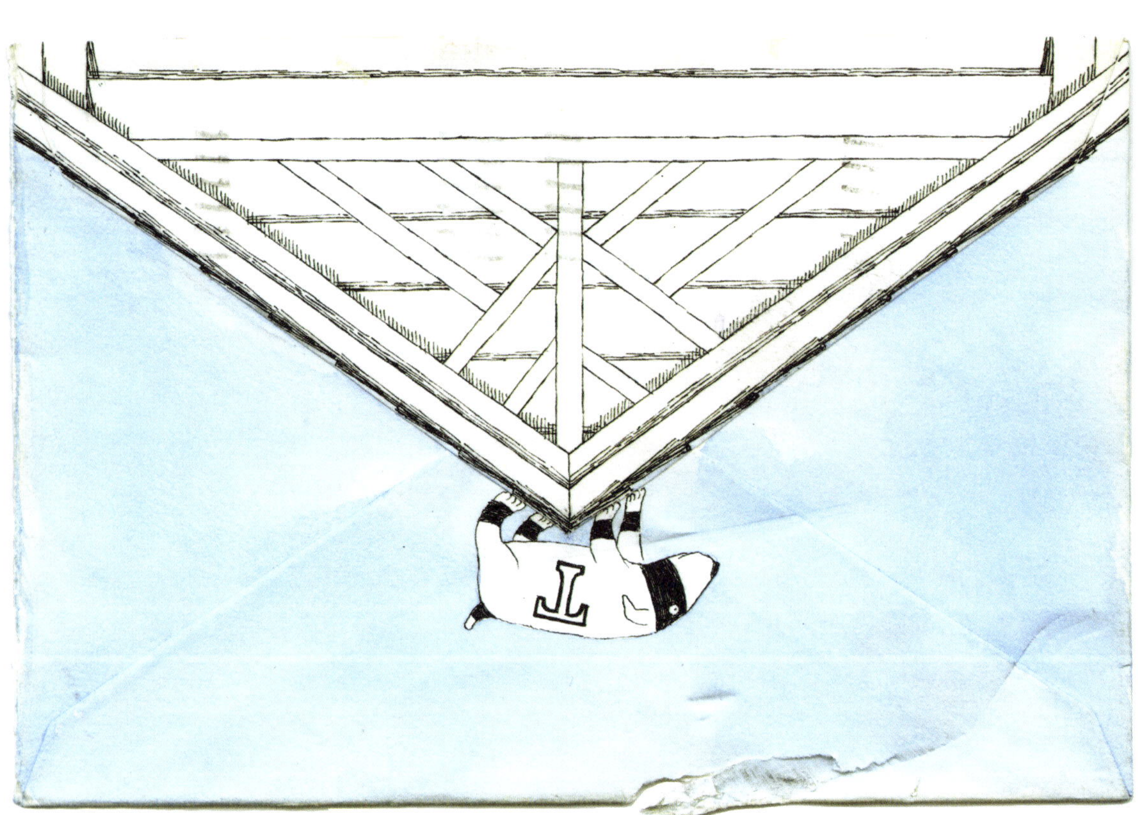

Morning, 8.vii.74

Dear Tom,

Your letter—all by itself in the mailbox—was a surprise, and ultimately, with its Ironical News, an unnerving one. But then what else is to be expected from Monday?

Our Fourth of July festivities were much as usual—watching fireworks the night before from the graveyard hill just up the road. Alas, there was no bonfire behind the general store as there had been for many years, and there were more people in the graveyard above ground than below—for the first time I think, but a tenuous continuity persists...

The cats say hello back.

Time is a horse that runs in the heart, a horse
Without a rider on a road at night.
The mind sits listening and hears it pass.

The Pure Good of Theory, WALLACE STEVENS

We hold these Truths...
UNITED STATES 10c
JUL 12
AM
1974
To
TOM FITZHARRIS
39 Hickory
Hill Road
10709
Eastchester,
New York

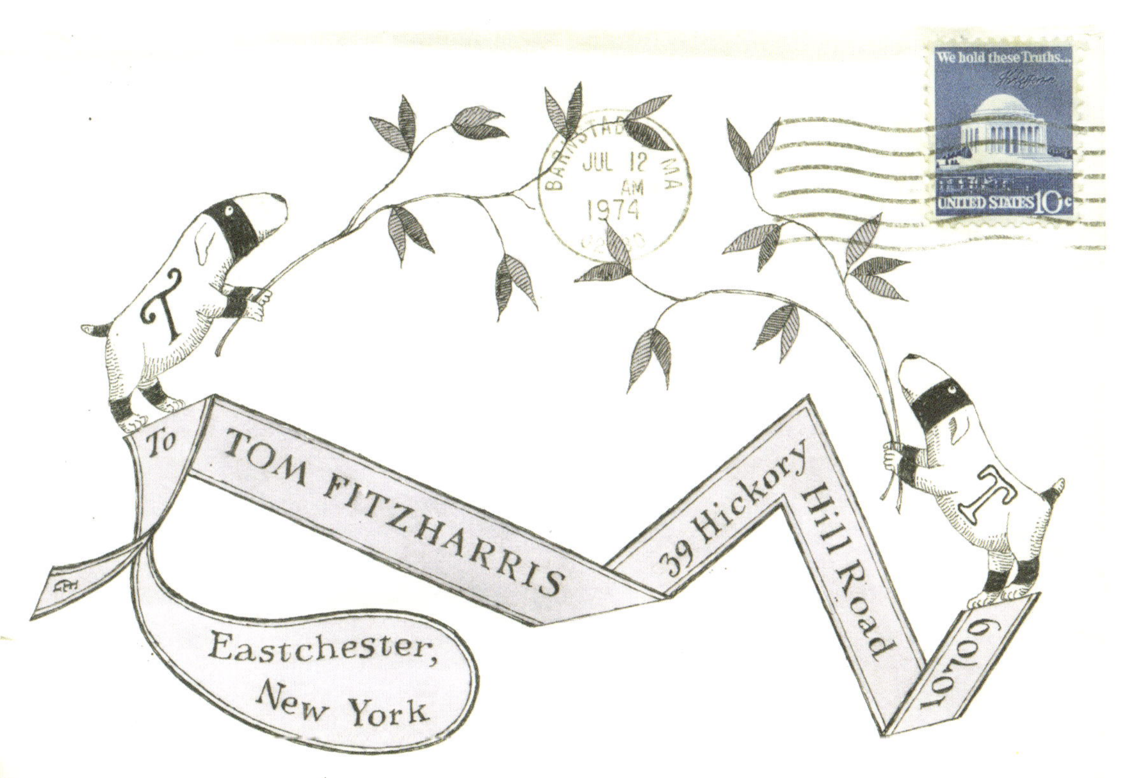

Two

Le plaisir délicieux et toujours nouveau d'une occupation inutile

HENRI DE REGNIER

(motto of Ravel's *Valses nobles et sentimentales*)

TOM FITZHARRIS
39 Hickory Hill Road
Eastchester, New York.
10709
We hold these Truths...
UNITED STATES 10c
PM
1974

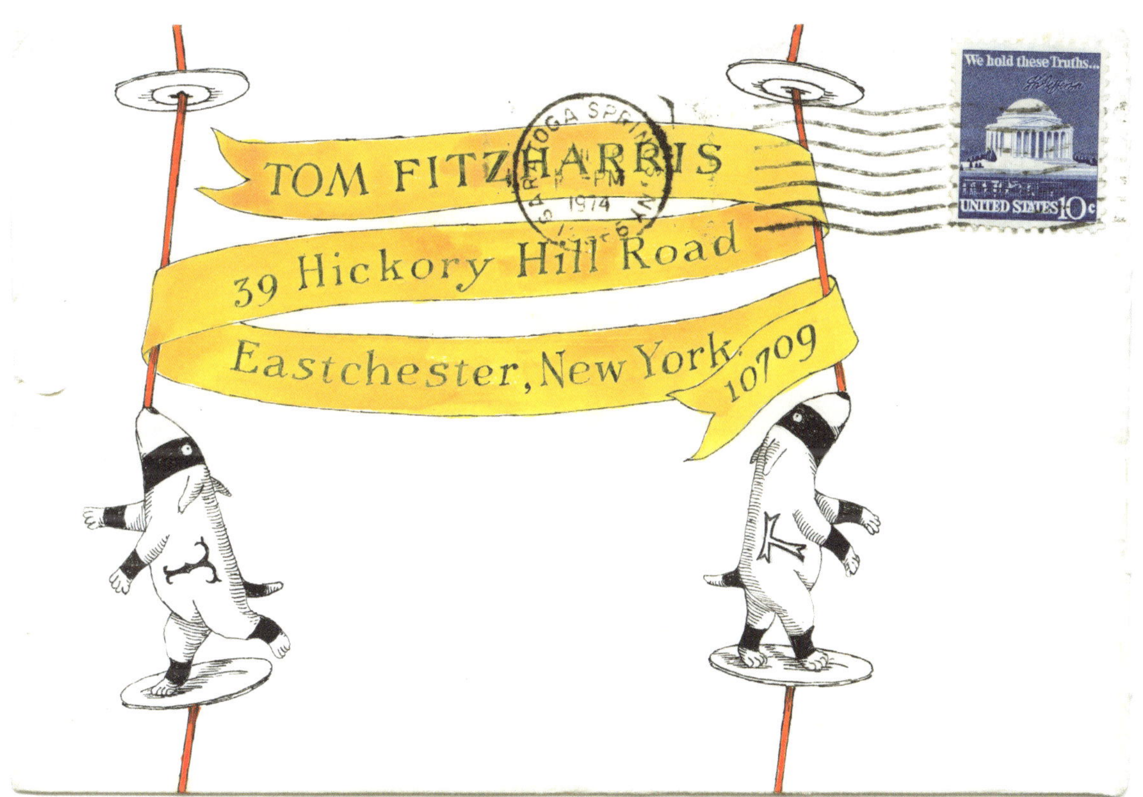

Three

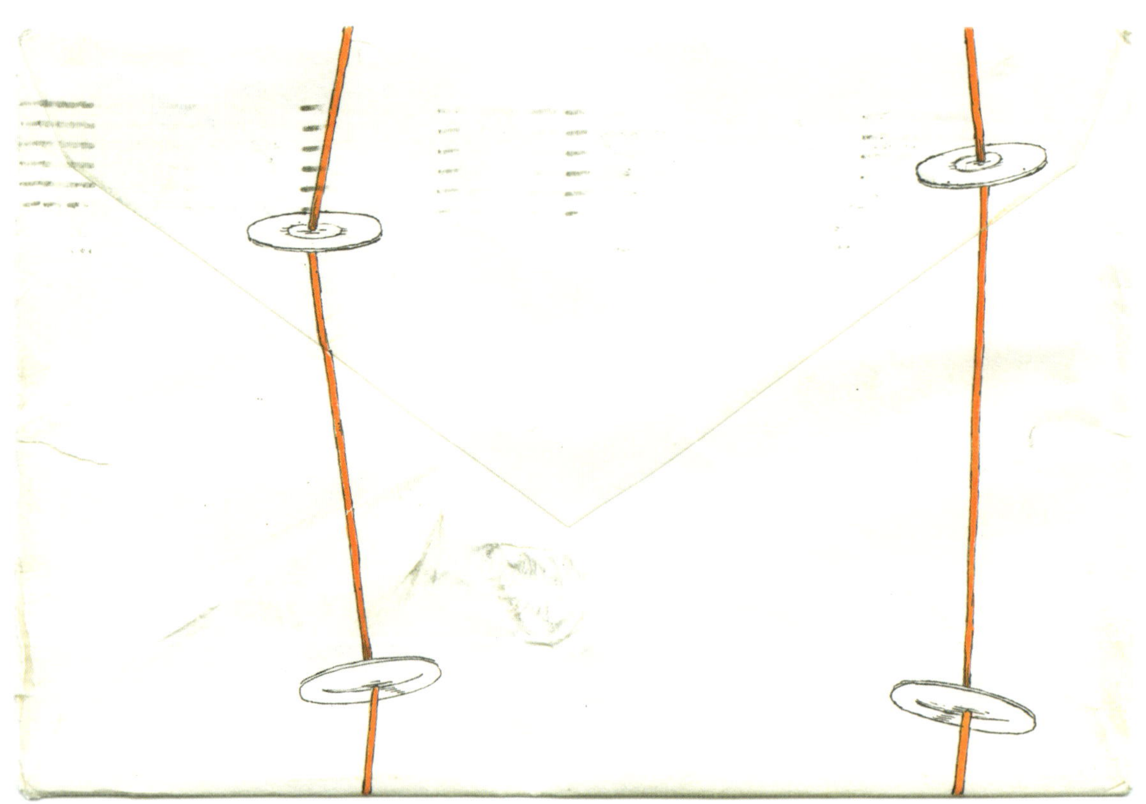

La vie toute faite de morceaux.
Sans suite comme des rêves.

GAUGUIN

TUESDAY MORNING

NO, I DID NOT DO THE ENVELOPE WHILE WATCHING THE DANCERS WARM UP, BUT AT MY OWN LITTLE DRAWING BOARD IN THE ATTIC BEFORE I LEFT.

AT THE MOMENT I'M SITTING IN FRONT OF A GULF STATION WAITING TO HAVE MY CAR INSPECTED, KNOCK WOOD.

THE WEATHER IS GORGEOUS, BUT THE INSECT LIFE THREATENS TO TAKE OVER AT ANY MOMENT.

AS DELIA PETERS WALKED OUT OF WARM UP BEING LEAD BY PETER MARTINS IN CLOGS YESTERDAY, SHE SAID: 'BORING!' 'OH' I SAID. 'I CAN'T STAND,' SHE SAID, 'DANISH PASTRY AT THIS TIME OF THE MORNING.' (AN ANECDOTE OF BALLET LIFE)

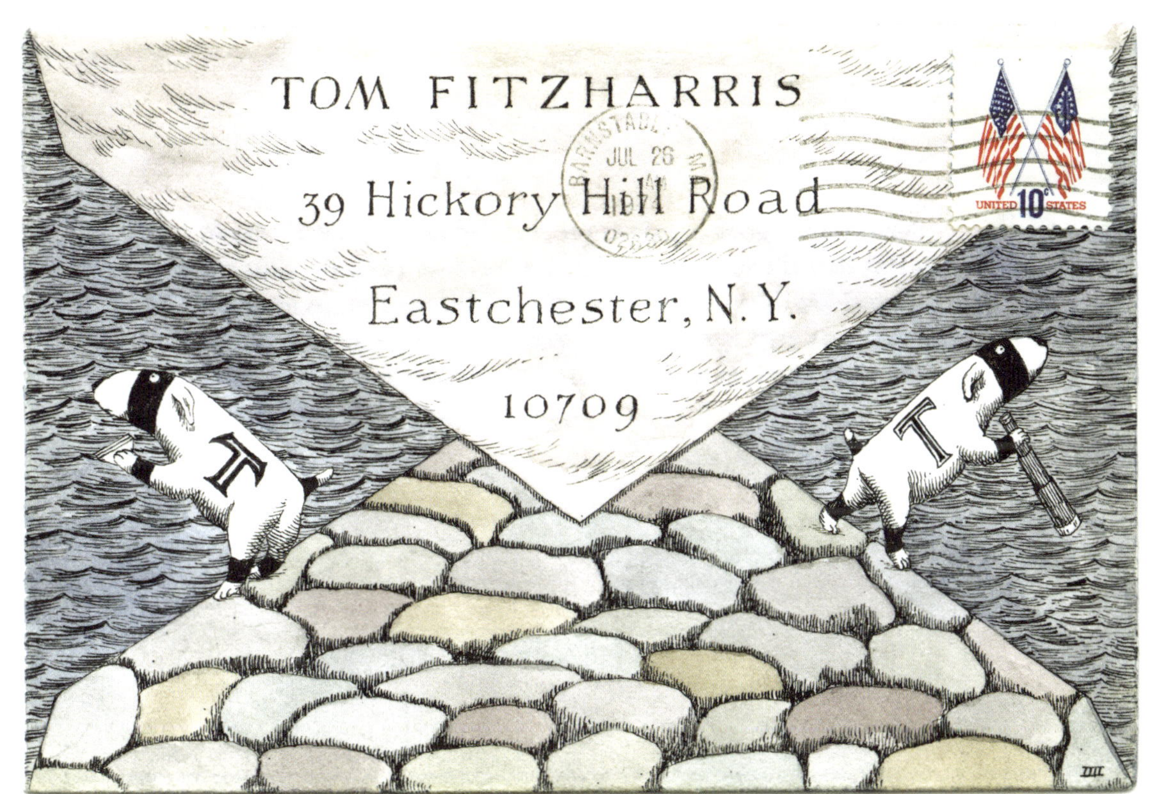
TOM FITZHARRIS
39 Hickory Hill Road
Eastchester, N.Y.
10709
JUL 26
UNITED 10c STATES

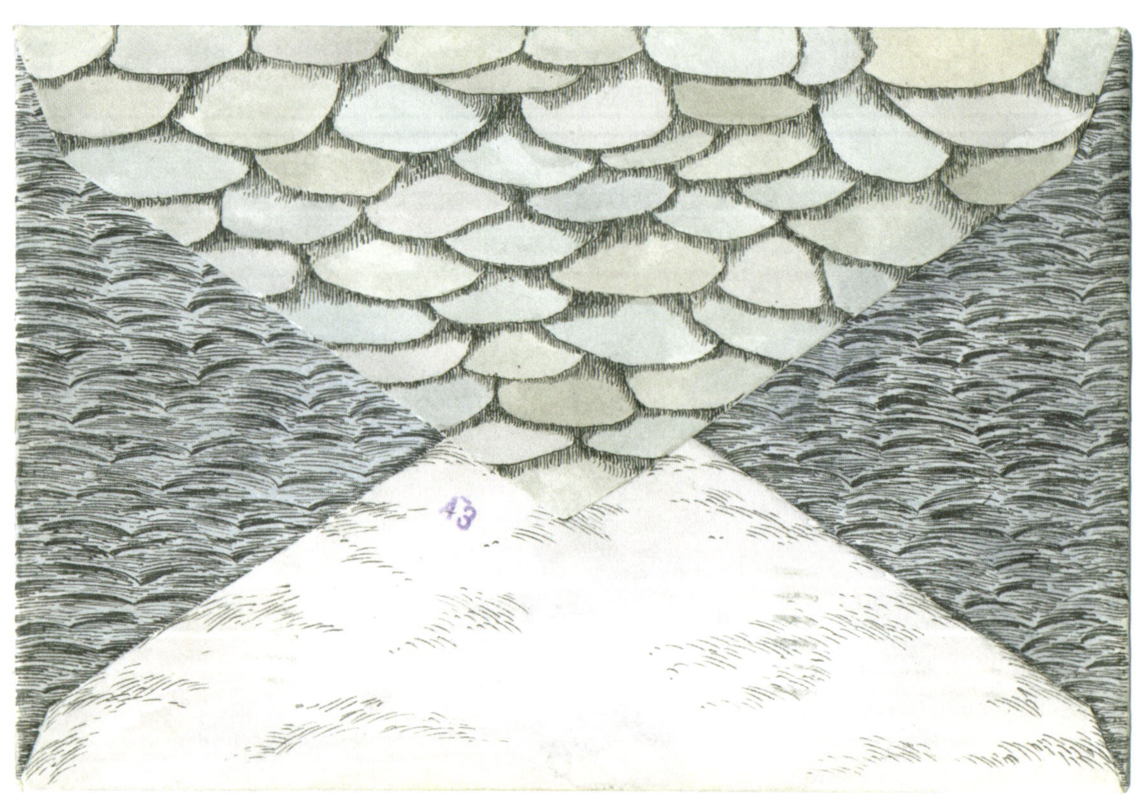
43

Music, states of happiness, mythology, faces belabored by time, certain twilights and certain places try to tell us something, or have said something we should not have missed, or are about to say something; this imminence of a revelation which does not occur is, perhaps, the aesthetic phenomenon.

BORGES

Thursday evening, 25.vii.74

Today I tried to accomplish something in various areas: success has been spasmodic.

2

Interim record report.

I was ravished by the Stephen Foster songs, especially Was my brother in the battle? Several tears narrowly escaped splashing on the envelope.

I'm now listening to the Sibelius Third Symphony. I don't care what you think.

3

The middle of the first movement of the Sibelius Fourth is even more splendidly mushy than the background music for Wuthering Heights, which it strongly resembles. This is known as Music Appreciation.

TOM FITZHARRIS
39 Hickory Hill Road
Eastchester
New York
10709
UNITED 10c STATES

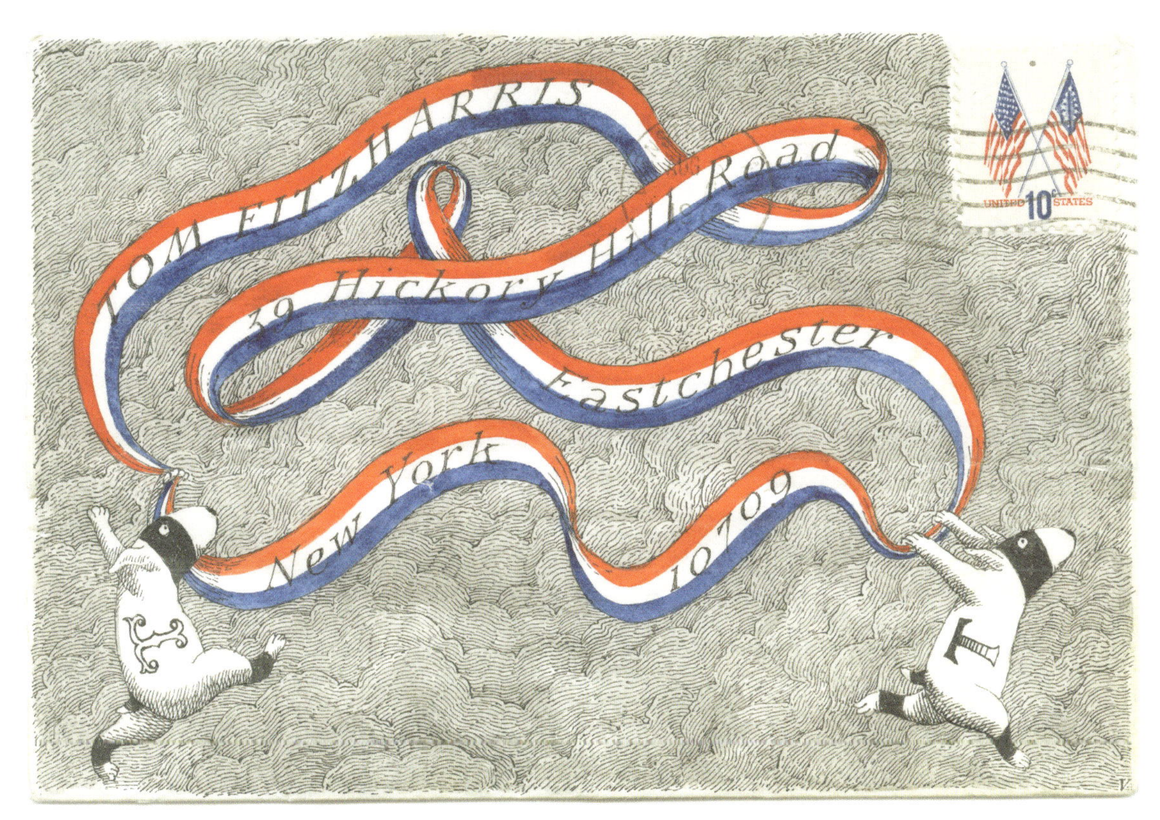

Five

But, after all, the whole *secret* of life is made up of the things one makes, and those one steals, and those one pays for.

ANNE THACKERAY RITCHIE

TOM
FITZ-
HARRIS
UNITED 10¢ STATES
39 Hickory Hill Road
New York
Eastchester
10709
VI

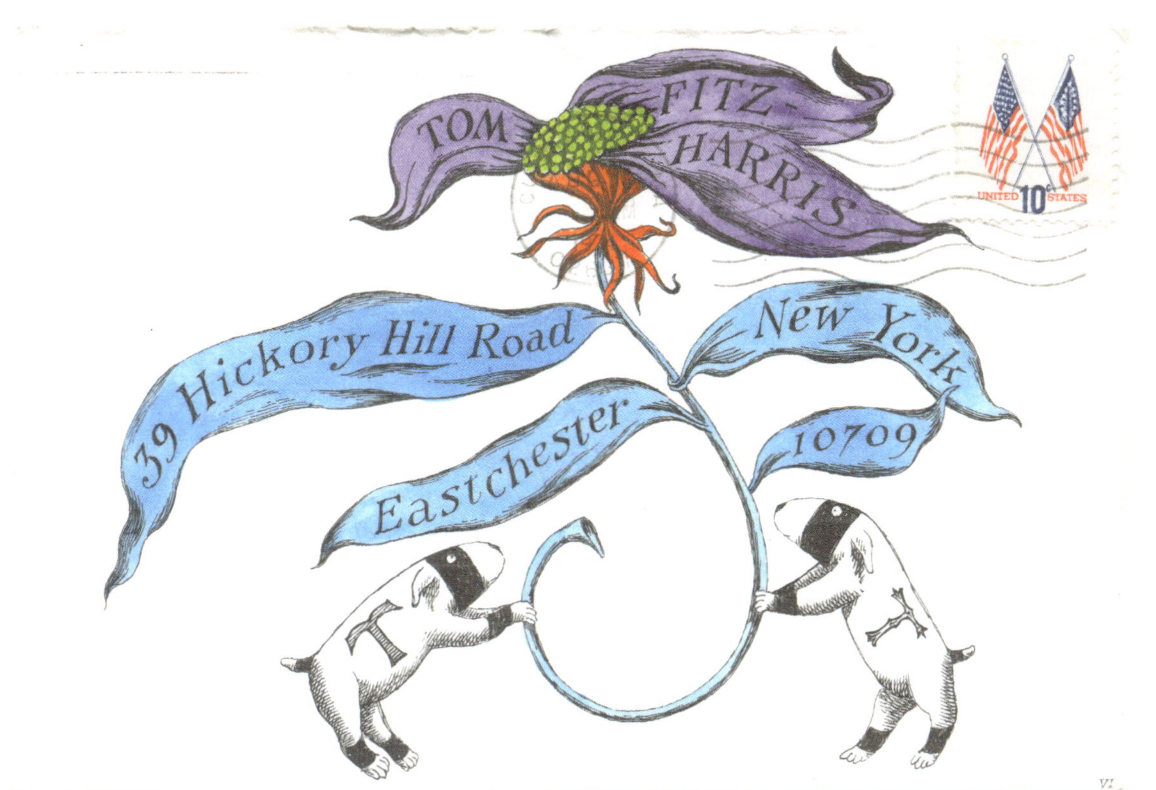

Six

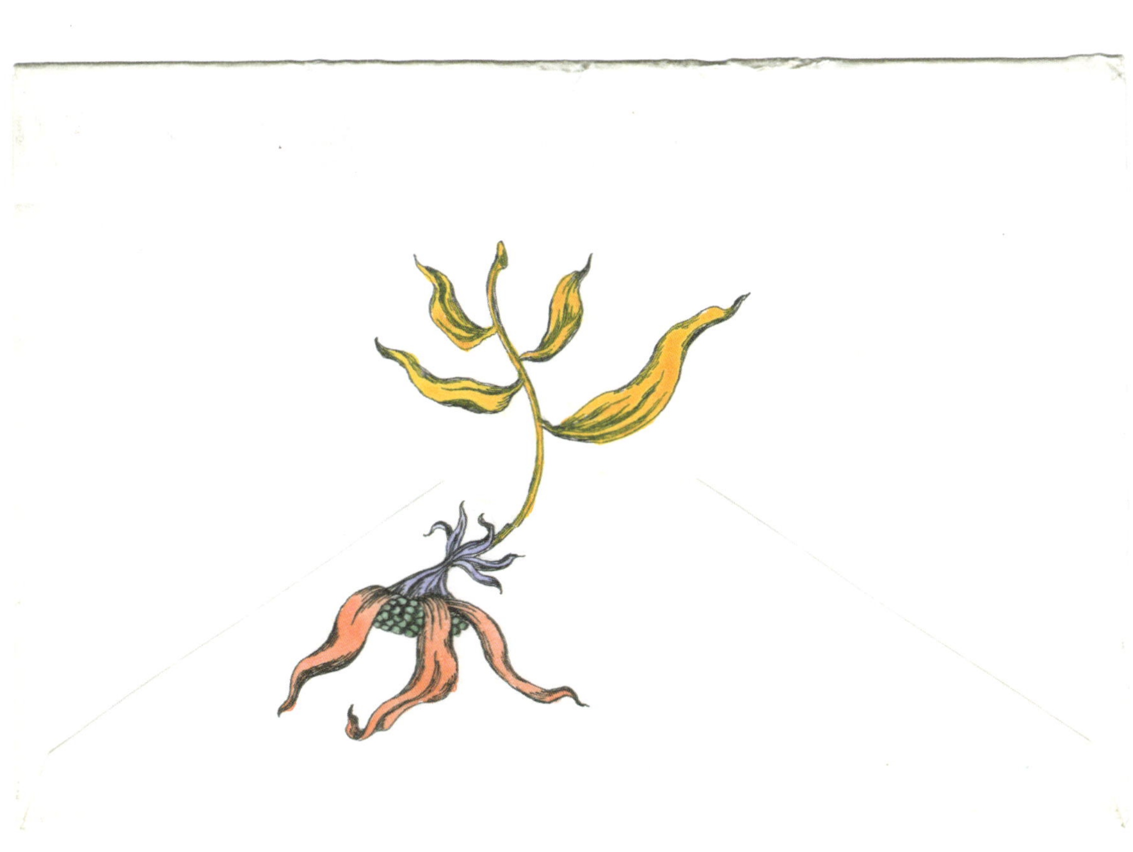

There is no truth; if there were, it could not be known; if known, it could not be communicated.

GORGIAS

Monday morning, 12.viii.74

I think I'll put this in the mail now, even if there is practically nothing in it, as the mails seem to be becoming more erratic and dilatory as the days go by.

I have a copy for you of The Rats of Rutland Grange, but I am far too lazy to bother mailing it at this point; I'm sure you can wait almost indefinitely.

Victorian Songs (Angel S-36975) I hope you will investigate--Excelsior may well be the great concert aria of its sort ever perpetrated. An absolutely perfect example of non-wobble. (Wobble I have dedided is what has been the matter with the world since roughly 1914; I'll try and explain what I mean sometime if you want.)

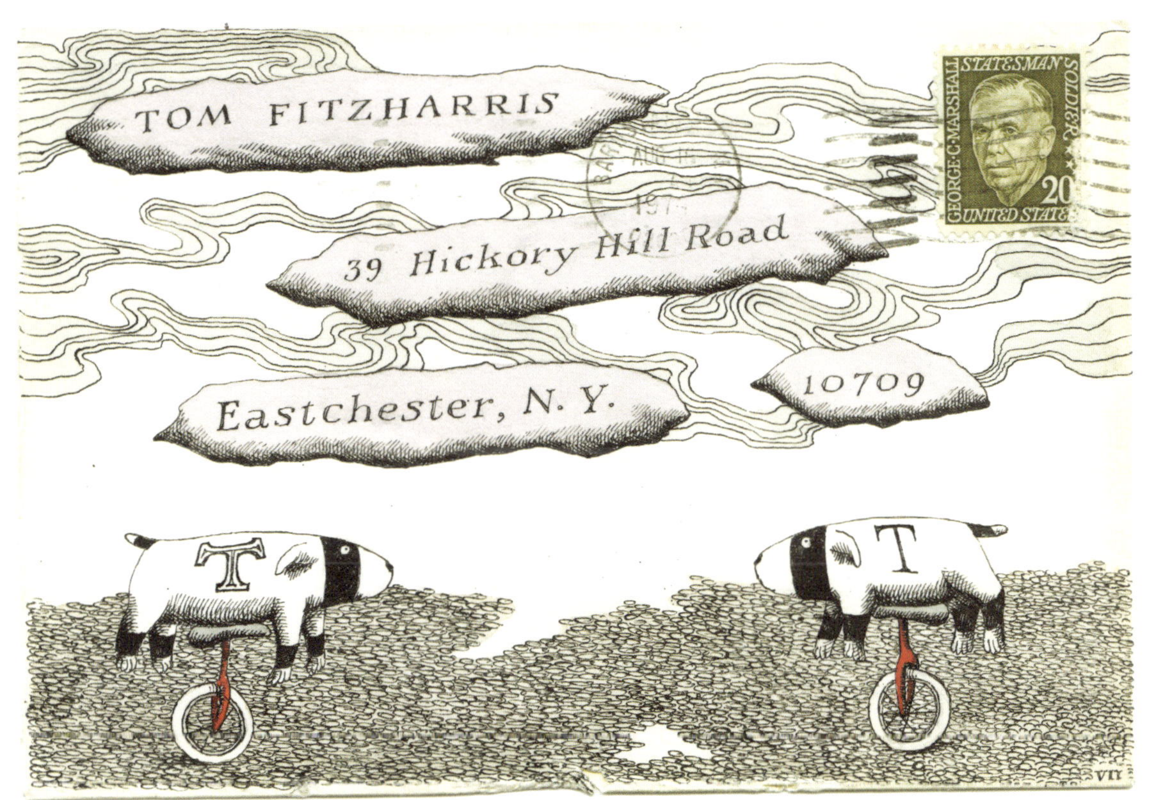
TOM FITZHARRIS
39 Hickory Hill Road
Eastchester, N.Y.
10709
STATESMAN
SOLDIER
GEORGE C. MARSHALL
20
UNITED STATES
T
T
VII

SOUTH SALEM, NY
AUG 19
AM
1974
10590

Thursday morning, 15.viii.74

I always felt the great crippling factor of my outlook or whatever was that I could never make it anything but esthetic; if only because it makes me wonder if I ever feel anything at all. After all, the world is not a picture or a book or even a ballet performance, not really.

In the meantime I am seriously considering cultivating stupidity, to the exclusion of everything else, as a way of life. I don't see why it won't work as well as anything else, and I have unlimited amounts at my disposal.

More of this eventually. I have to draw a crocodile in the sewers of Constantinople.

Les souvenirs sont cors de chasse
Dont meurt le bruit parmi le vent.

Memories are hunting horns
Whose sound dies out along the wind.

Apollinaire, trans. R. Shattuck

TOM FITZHARRIS
AUG 20
PM
1974
UNITED 10c STATES
TOM FITZHARRIS
39 HICKORY HILL ROAD
EASTCHESTER, N.Y. 10709
VIII

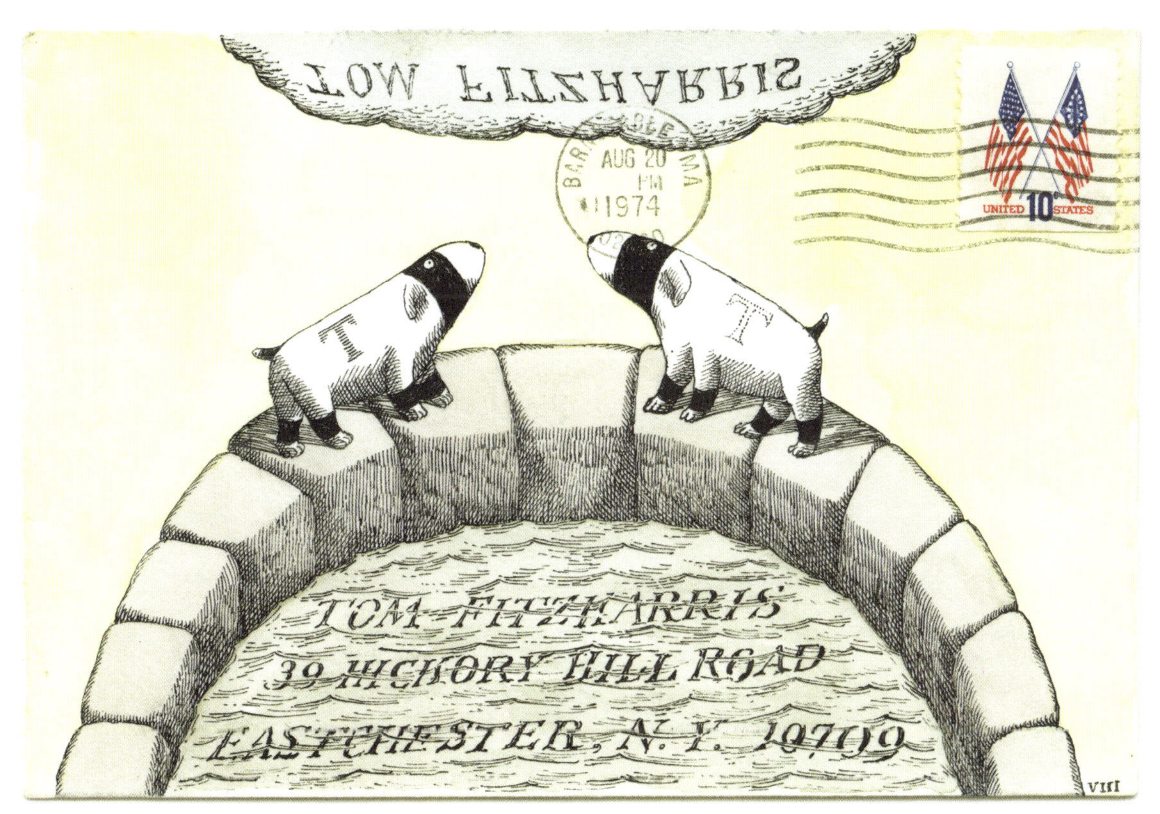

Eight

Tuesday afternoon

Several and a half dreary pages of this went into the wastebasket.

*

The art of being middle class consists in shutting yourself up in a detached house and only recognizing the people who come in at the front door.

G. F. Bradby

*

If one has romantic notions it is a clear sign that one is unequal to their fulfilment. People with interesting lives are all callous and brazen-faced. They feel nothing.

C.H.B. Kitchin, *Mr Balcony*

*

You might tell me about the spooky plants the English love.

I think I must be suffering from pre-Labor Day doom and gloom.

Sorry.

TOM FITZHARRIS
39 Hickory Hill Road
Eastchester
New York 10709
UNITED 10¢ STATES
IX

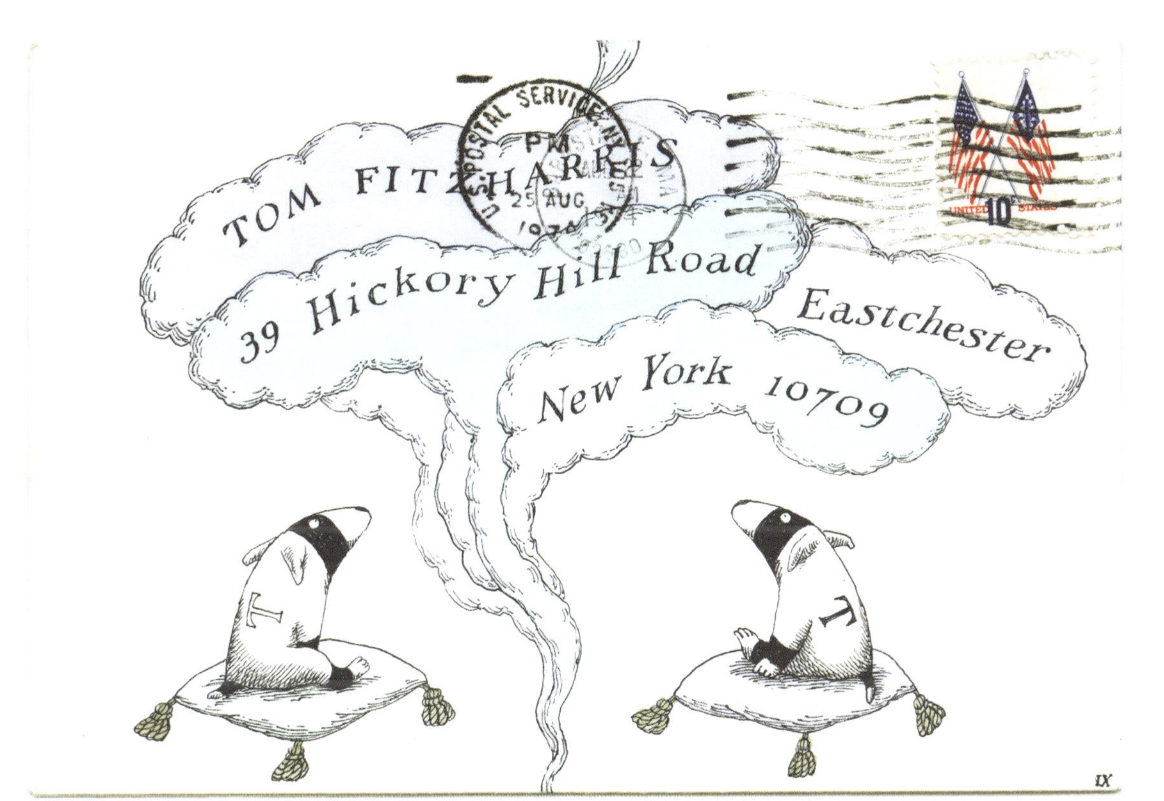

Nine

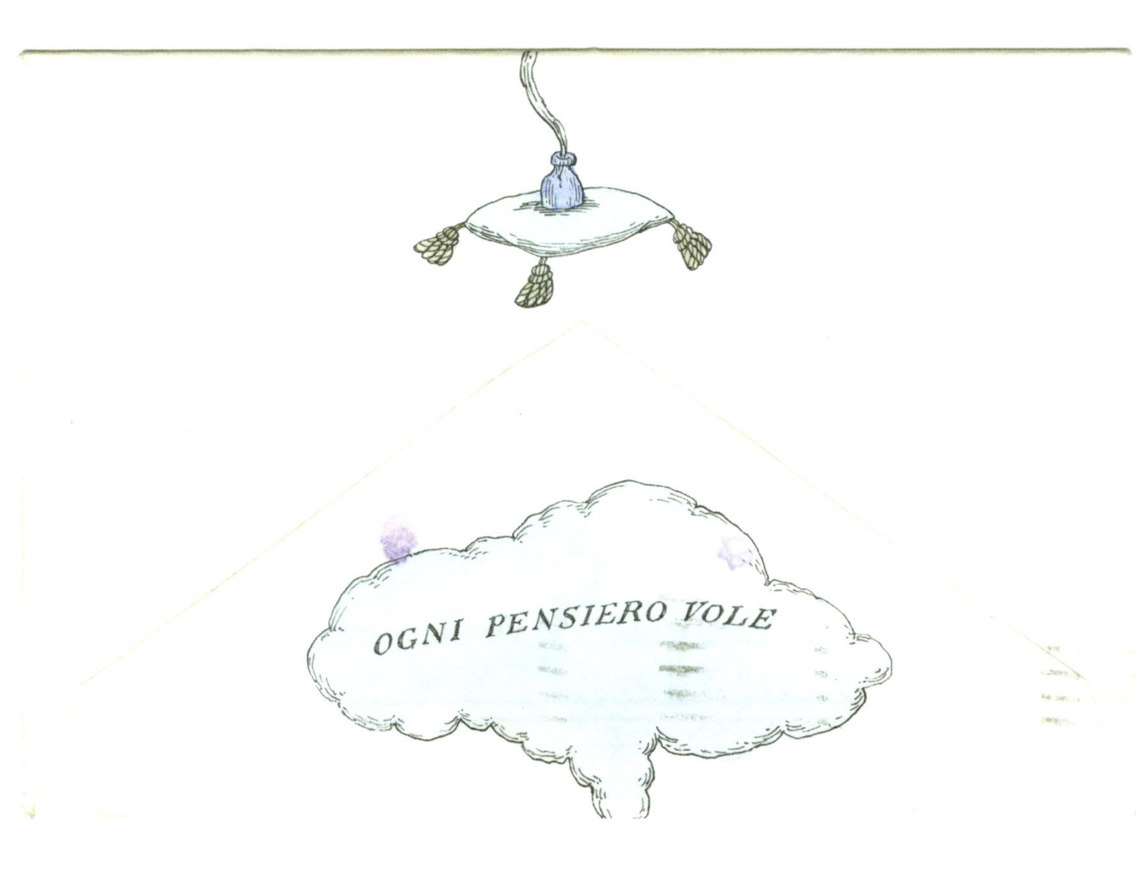
OGNI PENSIERO VOLE

Thursday morning, 22.viii.74

As Cocteau (or someone else maybe like that) said (in French, but I can't recall how it goes in that tongue): One has to be absolutely intransigent.

Do you feel M. Proust ever tells you anything you didn't know before? This is a serious question.

STATESMAN SOLDIER
GEORGE·C·MARSHALL
20c
UNITED STATES
Tom Fitzharris, 39 Hickory Hill Road, Eastchester, New York 10709

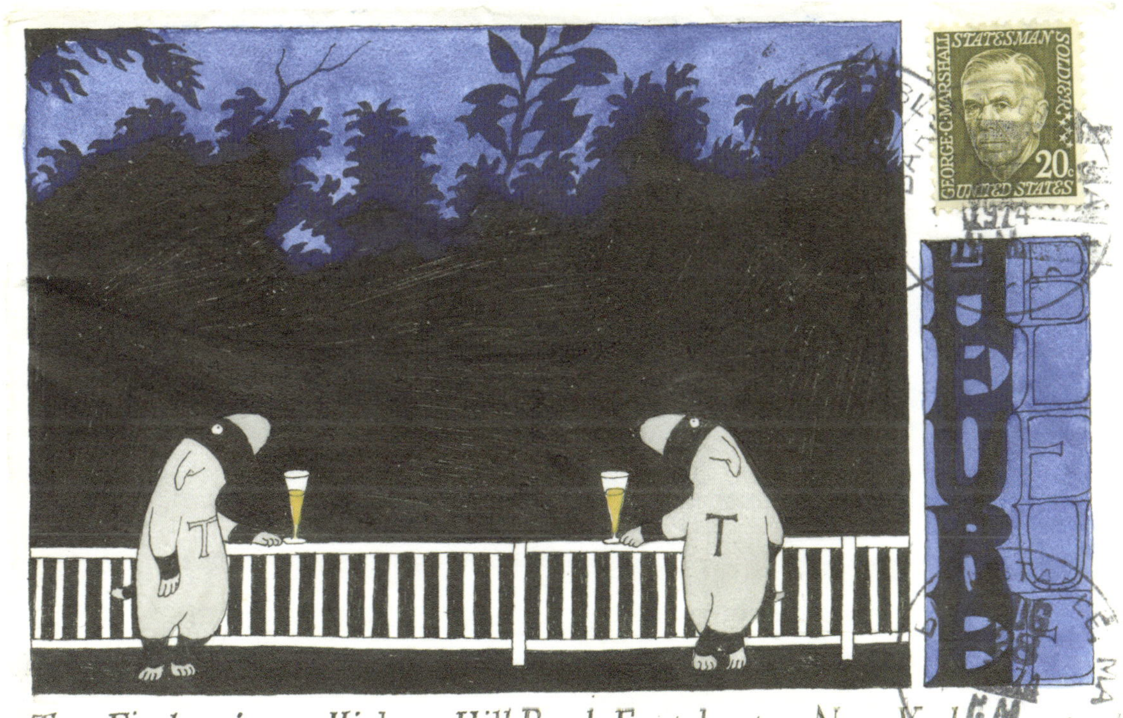

Ten

Indeed we are but shadows, we are not endowed with real life, and all that seems most real about us is but the thinnest shadow of a dream—till the heart be touched.

HAWTHORNE

26.viii.74, Monday evening

As I knew I would, I got slightly lost for about five minutes, but reached home about three. If it is any consolation to you, although I cannot think why it should be, I was up at eight-thirty so I probably did not get much more sleep than you did.

I trust you got home without mishap and unblinking headlights, or rather blinking ones.

Just before I went to bed as I was rattling cat food cans for my own upstairs, my cousin's ginger cat Alexander who had come home from the vet's in the interim appeared with a great gaping red hole in the centre of his rear back surrounded by a rectangle of shaven pink skin. (He had got an abscess from being in a fight.) It was a truly unnerving sight at that hour of the morning.

Although it's a revolting phrase yesterday was a happy day and I'm glad we did it; one cannot help but think how seldom in life one knows one is having one at the time.

There was some subject of high import I meant to deal with this morning, but I do not recollect what it was. I still haven't done the envelope. Time is passing. None of us is/are getting any younger. What does it all mean? We are temporarily out of oreos. Oh God.

It is not generally known that Mrs Regera Dowdy is the author of an (unwritten) very twee children's book entitled The Hollyhock That Looked in the Kitchen Window. It never will be written either.

It is getting even greyer and muggier if possible, and so am I. Yes. I desist...

Y(ours) E(ver)

HYANNIS, MA
SEP 2
PM
1974
UNITED 10c STATES
TOM FITZHARRIS
39 Hickory Hill Road
Eastchester, New York
10709
T
T
XI

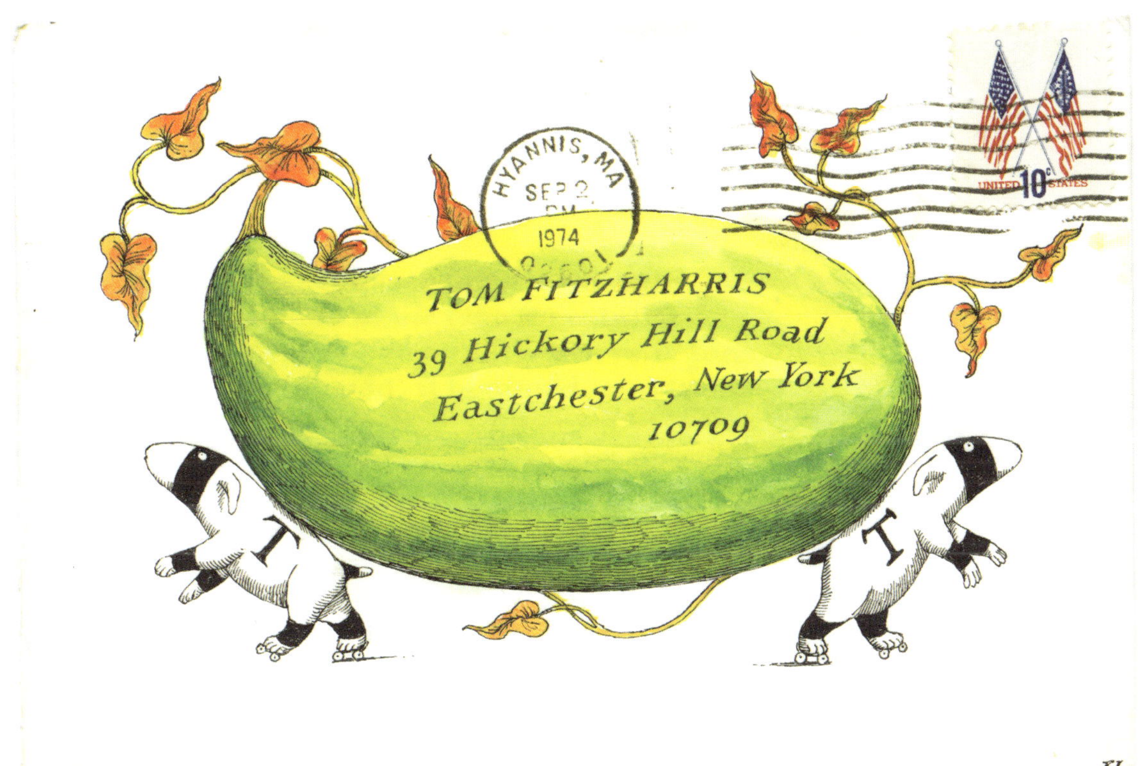

Eleven

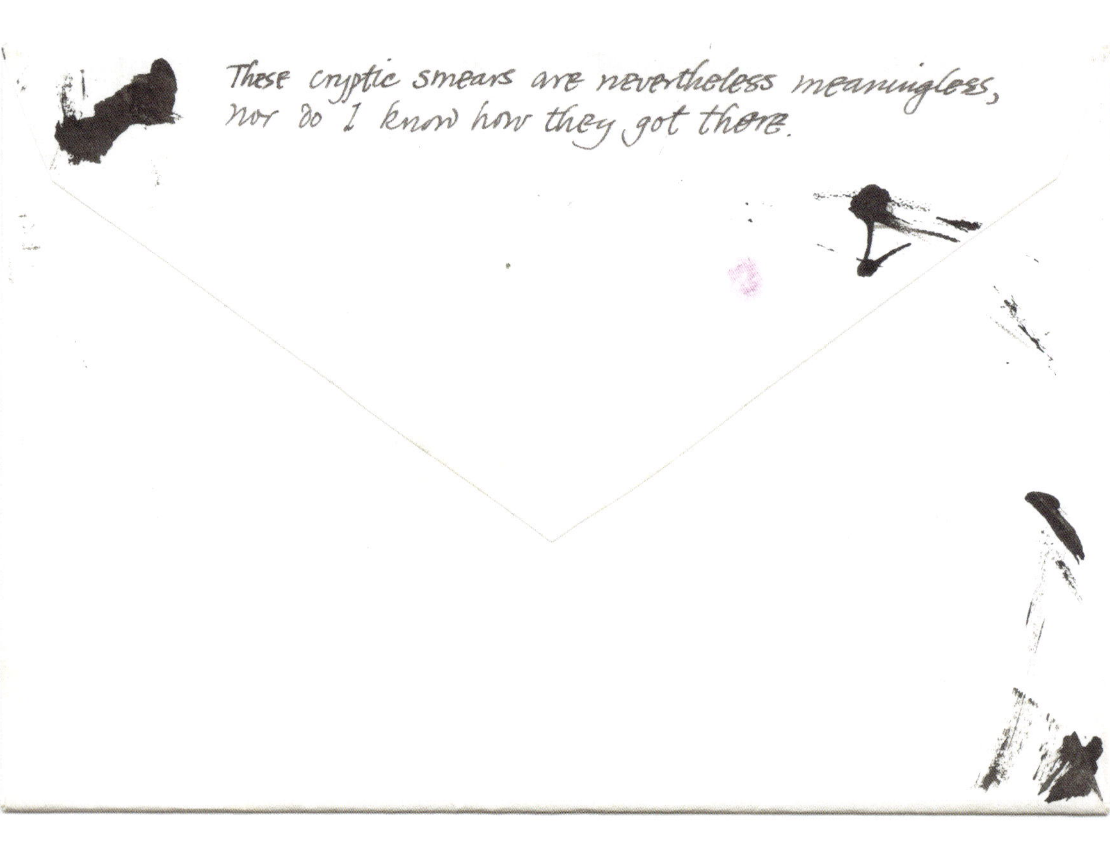
These cryptic smears are nevertheless meaningless,
nor do I know how they got there.

A very queer thing is the wind
I don't know how it beginn'd
And nobody knows where it goes,
It is wind, it beginn'd, and it blows.

THE MIDNIGHT FOLK, *John Masefield*

STATESMAN SOLDIER
UNITED STATES
20c
HYANNIS, MA
SEP 8
PM
1974
T
T
Tom Fitzharris, 39 Hickory Hill Road, Eastchester, New York 10709 XII

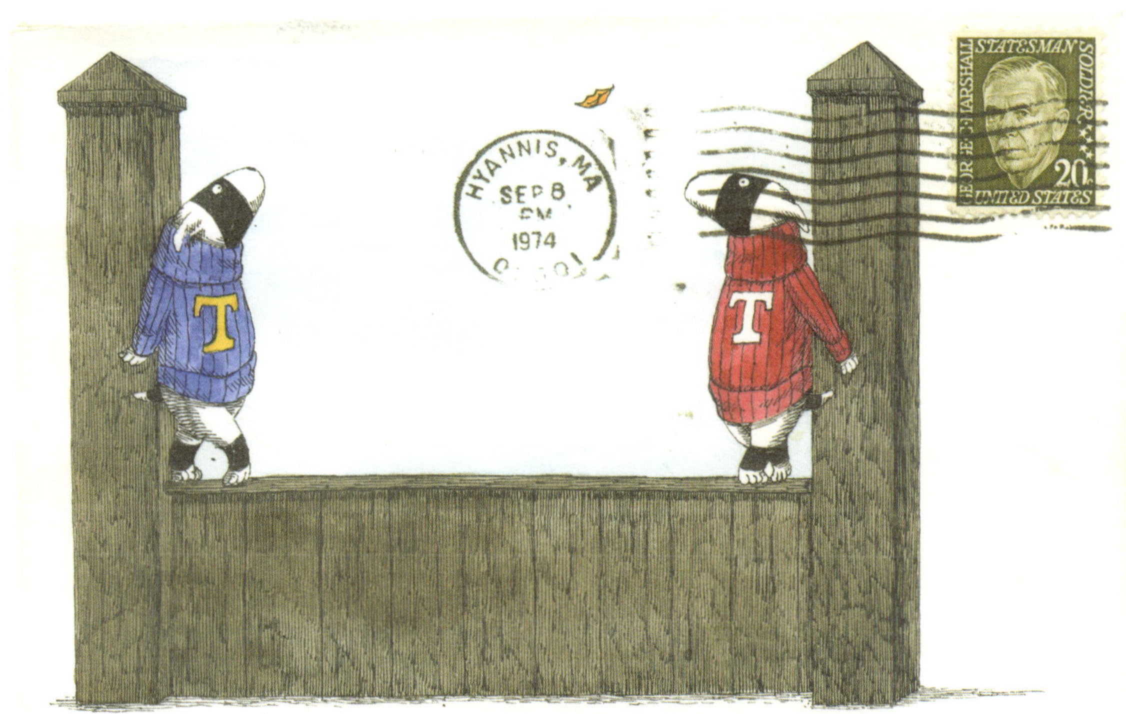

Twelve

This envelope is pretty twee. If you don't want to stop for dinner, we are accustomed to supplying large amounts of food to arrivals far into the night. (This remark supplements end of letter.)

'... And what's dust-bins? Glass bottles, mostly, what's empty. What's dust-heaps? Old tins what's been under the tap. And what's life? That's what.'

THE MIDNIGHT FOLK, *John Masefield*

Life being what it is, one dreams of revenge.

GAUGUIN

Friday night, 30.viii.74

The Labor Day weekend has already become a sort of nightmare, although none of its aspects are worth going into.

Saturday morning

The weather seems to have improved. I have already made a meatloaf, boiled a lot of eggs hard preparatory to devilling them, and there is a loaf of walnut cheese bread hopefully baking in the oven. I say hopefully as the dough was very peculiar indeed.

Monday morning

At the rate I'm (not) functioning, you will be lucky to receive this letter this week.

I spent yesterday in the kitchen in preparation for having various non-resident cousins to dinner; the turkey had a stuffing that contains thirty-one ingredients and by the time I had the whole thing together, I felt so disenchanted with the whole thing that I went off and had supper at the Friendly's in Hyannis.

That you will be reading this probably on Tuesday conjures up images of impassable glaciers of time. I have no confidence that I'll still be alive by then.

I made a frog today that I shall leave you in my will if I ever get around to making one. A certain small object has, along with the usual rice, been sewed up inside it.

TOM FITZHARRIS
39 Hickory Hill Road
Eastchester
New York
10709
UNITED STATES 10c
SEP 12 1974 A.M.

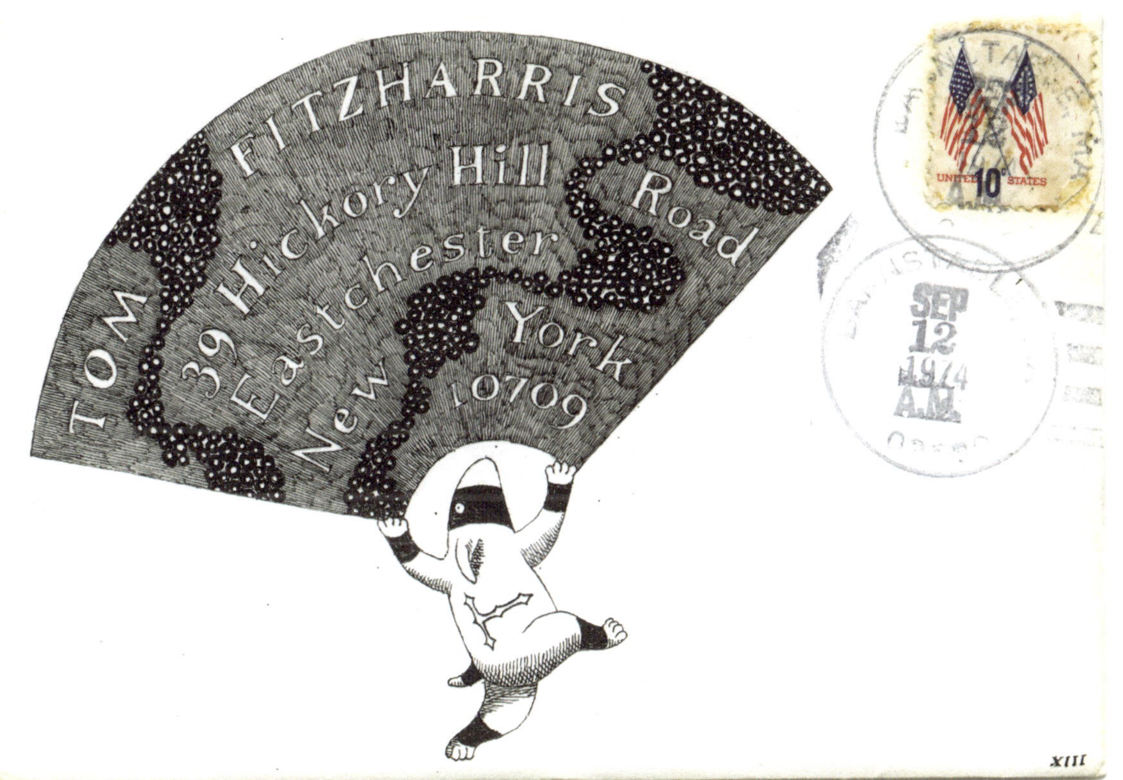

Thirteen

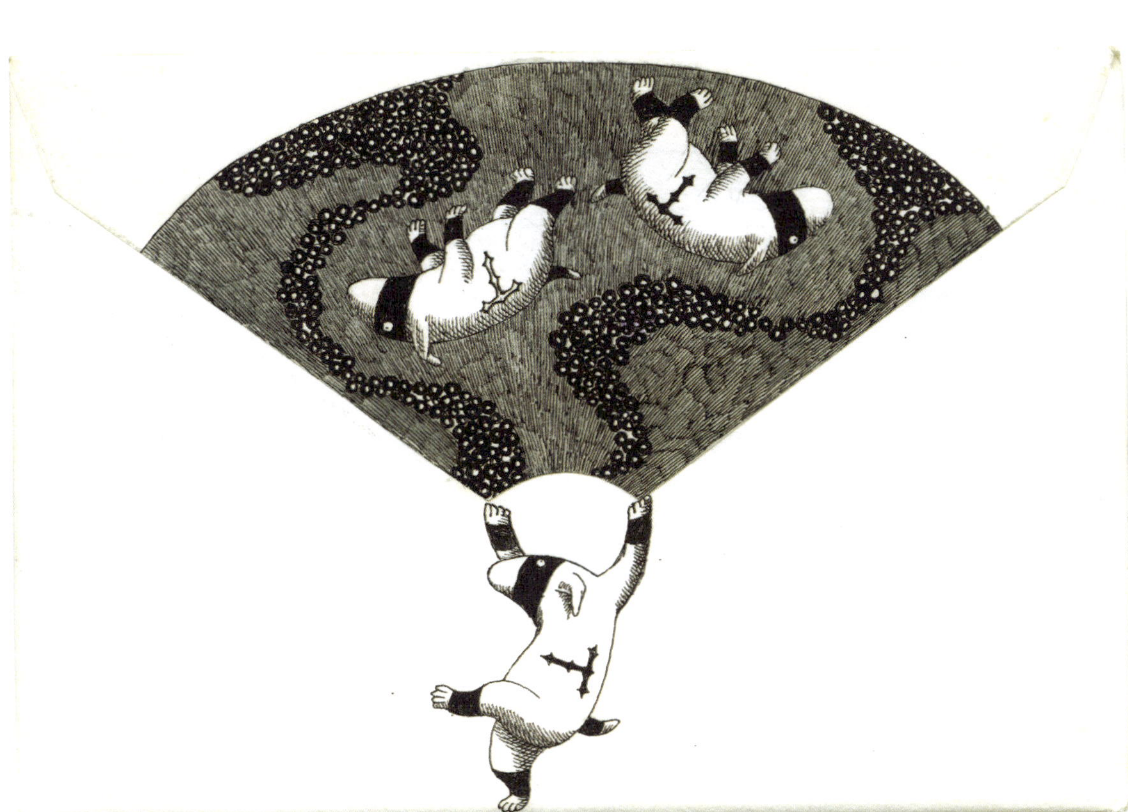

One's intentions make life nearly unendurable.

Everything we come across is to the point.

JOHN CAGE

Friday morning, 6.ix.74

Doing anything to postpone drawing and writing letters I have filled the attic with cranberry packing crates and filled them with books and records. The attic is now very tidy--for the attic. Since you know my apartment, you can guess what I mean.

In my forwarded-from-New-York mail were three NYCB subscriptions. My heart sank. It sinks very easily these days. It is sunken most of the time.

But let us not close on a depressed note.

Tra la.

I assume, more or less, you'll be here sometime Friday evening--arrive in time for dinner if by any chance you can get started earl~~ier~~y enough--unless I hear something to the contrary.

TOM
FITZHARRIS
39 Hickory Hill Road
Eastchester, New York
10709
STATESMAN SOLDIER
GEORGE C. MARSHALL
20c
UNITED STATES
XIII (Sic

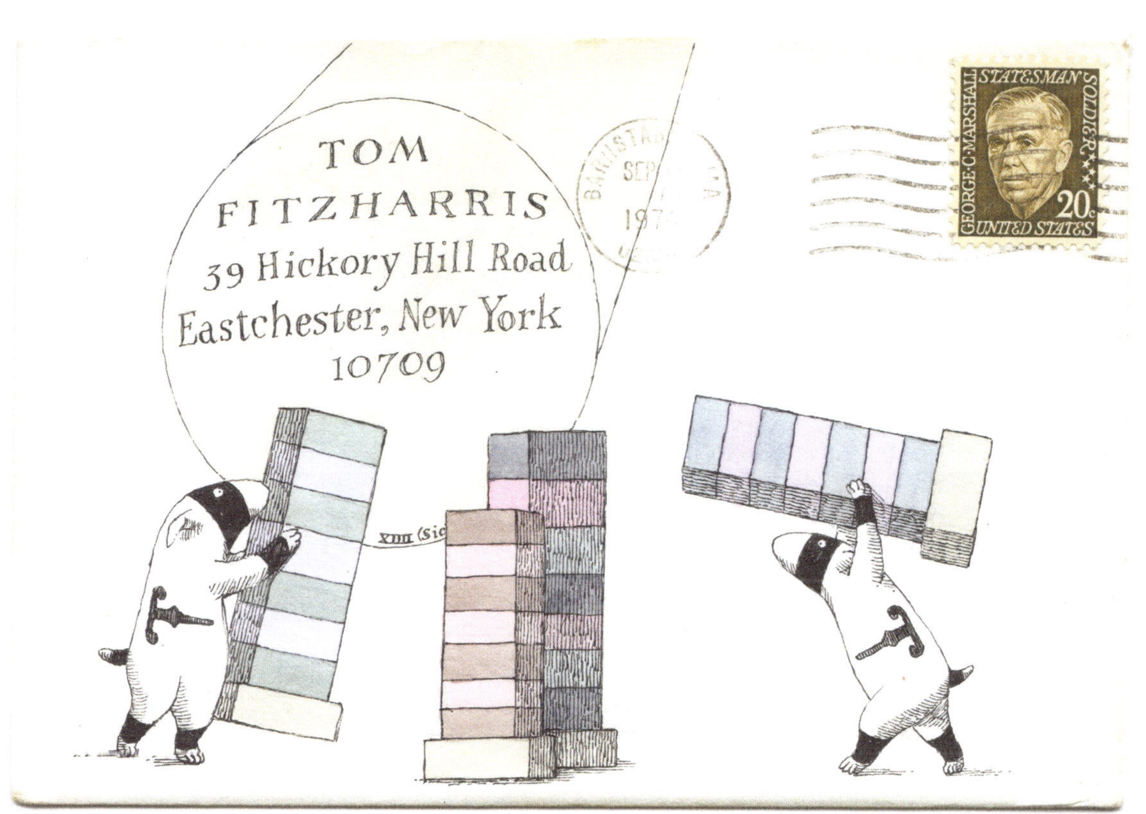

Fourteen

There in the sky,
Where the paths of summer and autumn cross,
A cooling wind will blow from many sides.

KOKIN SHŪ

Monday night, 16.ix.74

After the weekend I am finding it very difficult to come off the boil as it were.

As I always find it impossible to stay in the house after the departure of house guests, I went out driving for the rest of the afternoon which grew more golden and perfect as it went on. Everything presented itself to view as a possible Fitzharris photograph. In Sandwich I found a Rover Boys book I was missing, along with several other books, and a large grey wooden masher of some sort which looks like an extremely elegant piece of modern sculpture. Pushing on, I discovered that my favourite antique shop, in Forestdale, had not gone out of business at the end of last summer as I had been led to suppose, so that was a pleasant surprise; there I got a small lavender plate that looks well in the living room, a bit of carved wood, a sort of irregular panel, that came from heaven only knows what, and a couple of other oddments I can't remember--oh yes, two small mercury glass doorknobs.

Tuesday morning

Everything I suppose sorts itself out. At the moment I feel I may pop.

I hang on firmly to the fact that Life is full of alternatives but no choice (Patrick White) because if I felt I had any control over my flying off in all these new directions all of a sudden and at once, I should obviously feel that I oughtn't to, because what I really should be doing is narrowing my interests, etc, etc. and further disciplining my work, which is what I have been trying to do, but then one can't really escape life so there's no point in bothering about trying, and if everything gets messier and more untidy and all the rest of it, well, that's how it is.

Johann Christian Bach's Six Symphonies for Wind are to die.

Today I rushed off to the Market Bookshop in Falmouth figuring they would probably have the best stock of photography books around, and ran amuck there, and later on at Parnassus and the Paperback Booksmith ditto on a smaller scale.

I picked up: the Szarkowski Looking at Photographs , which I have gone through completely if rapidly; the Meatyard monograph and his Family Album of Lucybelle Crater, which latter a hasty perusal of makes me think one of the photographs, any one of them, makes the point, and all the rest are repetition, but I may change my mind later; otherwise (damn this ribbon which does not reverse itself without help), Frank's The Americans; Travelog by Charles Harbutt; Sequences by Duane Michals,(these I recollect with a certain amount of dubious pleasure from the MOMA); Imogen Cunningham; Clarence John Laughlin; Aperture 13:4 and 16:1; Rural Maine by Mark Silber; Ansel Adams' Singular Images; Riding the Rails by Michael Mathers; A Country Camera 1844-1914 by Gordon Winter (Penguin); Art and Photography by Aaron Scharf (Pelican); and Sun Pictures, the Hill-Adamson calotypes by David Bruce. This should keep me busy. I also picked up John Cage's Silence and M, and Fuller's Spaceship Earth thing, as I figured I ought to read at least one of them if I am going to continue with Mr Cage.

STATESMAN
SOLDIER
GEORGE C. MARSHALL
20c
UNITED STATES
SEP
20
1974
Tom Fitzharris, 39 Hickory Hill Road, Eastchester, New York 10709
xv

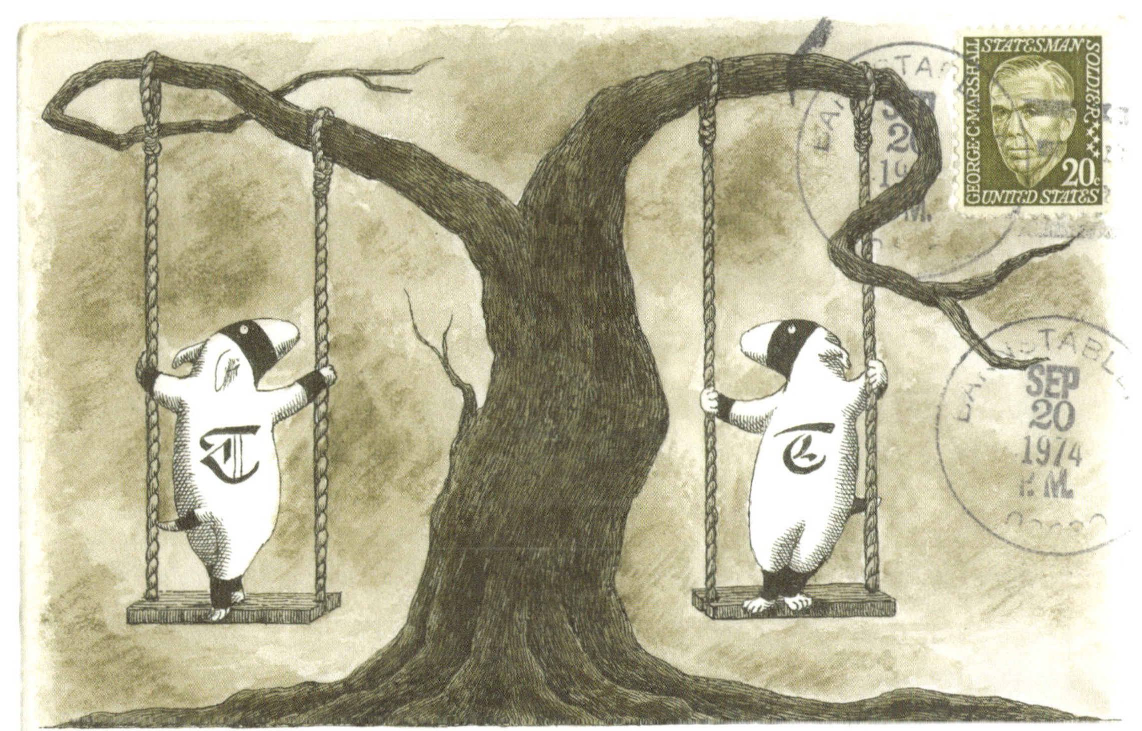

Fifteen

Every scene, even the commonest, is wonderful, if only one can detach oneself, casting off all memory of use and custom, and behold it (as it were) for the first time.

ARNOLD BENNETT, *Journal*, January 11, 1897

M r R Mitchell Dr.

To the ELM ST. M. E. CHURCH, for Rent of 2 Seats

in Pew No. 83 from Sept to December

1858 Received Payment, 2 25

G. THOMPSON,

for Committee.

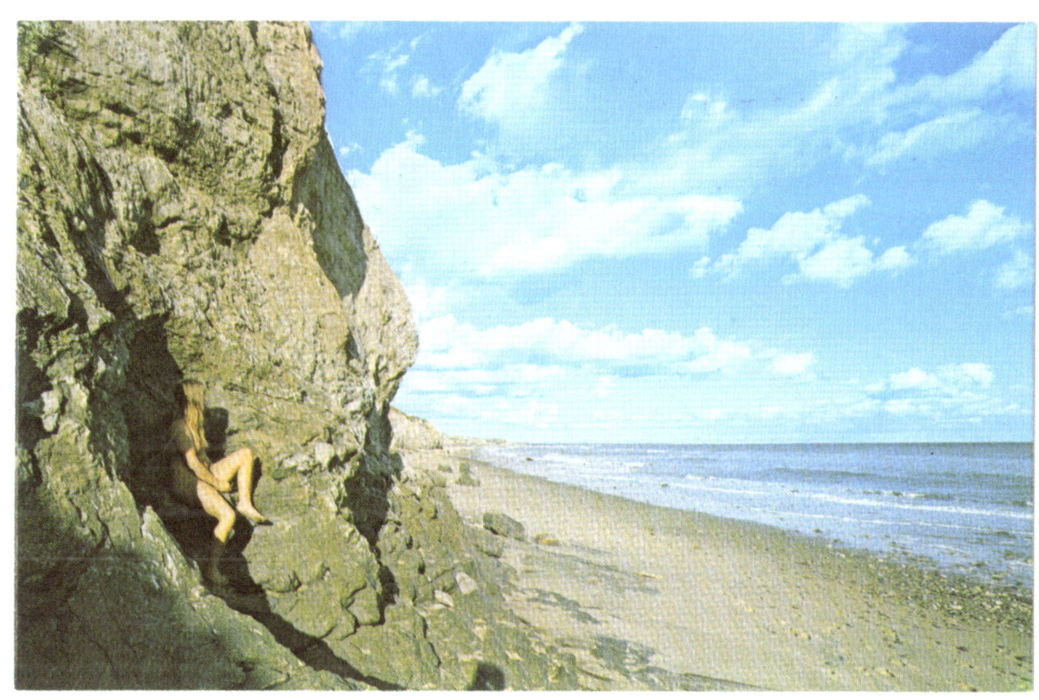

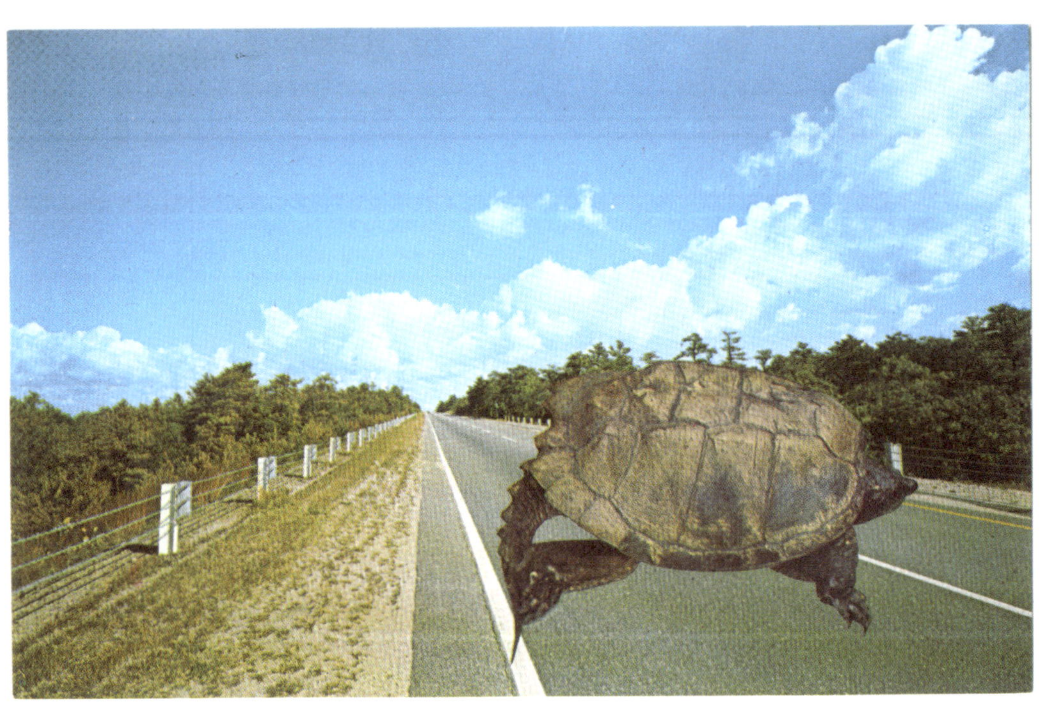

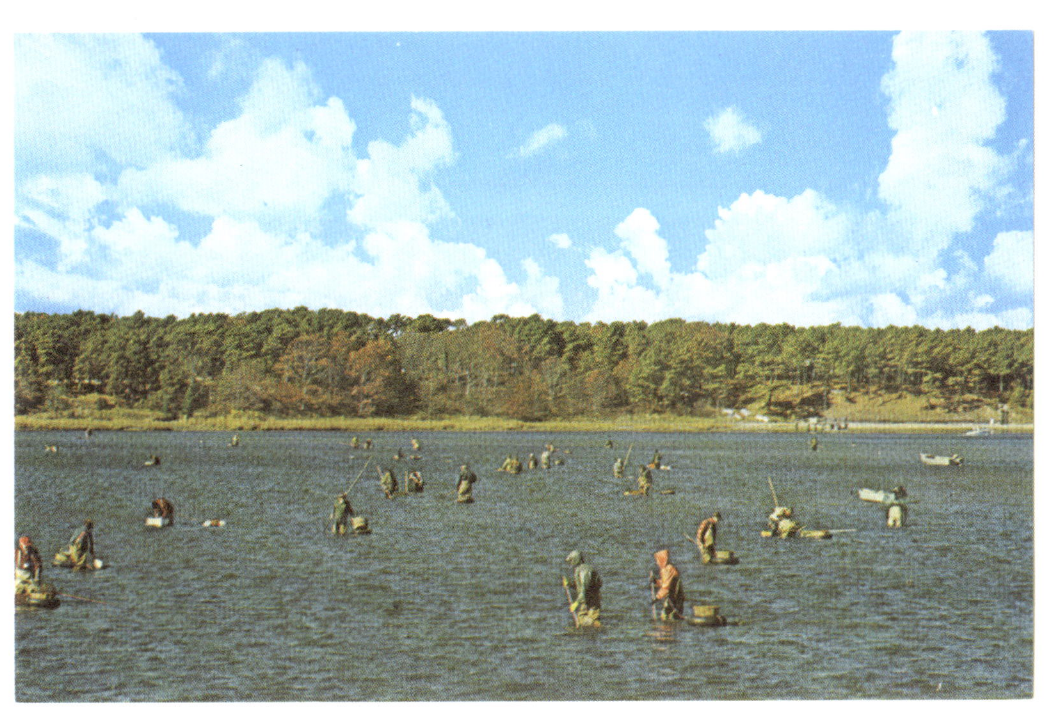

Wednesday morning, 18.ix.74

I *insist* on showing you the next time you're here the house where Kurt Vonnegut *used* to live.

*

I did *not* send your Stereo Reviews back first class. Let me know when you *don't* get them.

*

I don't *think* I bought anything you could get half off on. Or did I?

*

Would you *consider* taking photographs of me? This way if you don't want to, it does not have to be further *mentioned*.

*

I must do some *work*.

I am amassing a list of books to ask Burt Britton at Strand to dig up and hold for me; what else may you have in mind besides the Sendak Grimm?

(end of Wednesday)

Thursday afternoon

I think you will find the enclosed postcards (which I could not bring myself to send unenveloped through the mail) more something (I doubt if the word is 'meaningful') if you regard them as being a triptych. But then again.

(end of Thursday)

Black gloom however has set in as a result, though perhaps of something else. Why am I telling you this?

Thursday morning

This has turned into one of those weeks where I am getting things done that in size are no larger than a pea. I expect at the end of it they will then all spill and roll away into ungetatable cracks.

*

My cats are in a mysterious state, rushing about in a frantic manner. I sit at the typewriter and drawing board.

*

Yesterday I bought a terrific unsittablein chair which the man was delivering this morning, but he hasn't.

*

ove one anoth

(This comes from something I'll show you when you're next here. Though it can be explained, it needs to be seen for best effect.)

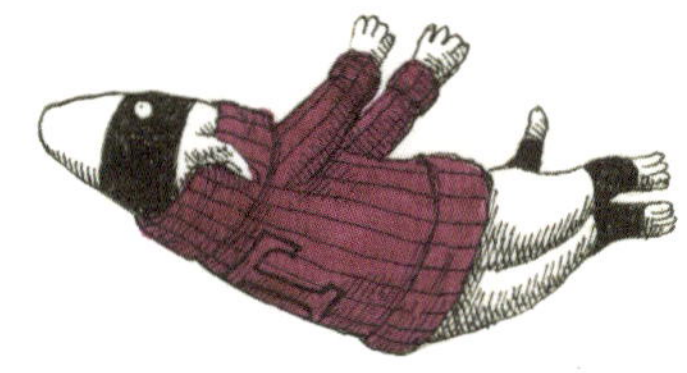

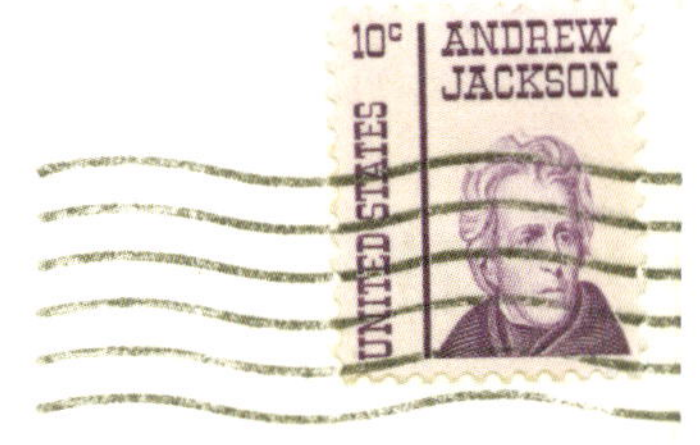

TOM FITZHARRIS,
39 Hickory Hill Road,
Eastchester,
New York.
10709.

Sixteen

Many a mad magenta moment
Lights the lavender of life

SANDYS WASON

BARNSTABLE, MA
SEP 25
AM
1974
02630
UNITED STATES
10c
Tom Fitzharris, 39 Hickory Hill Road, Eastchester, New York 10709

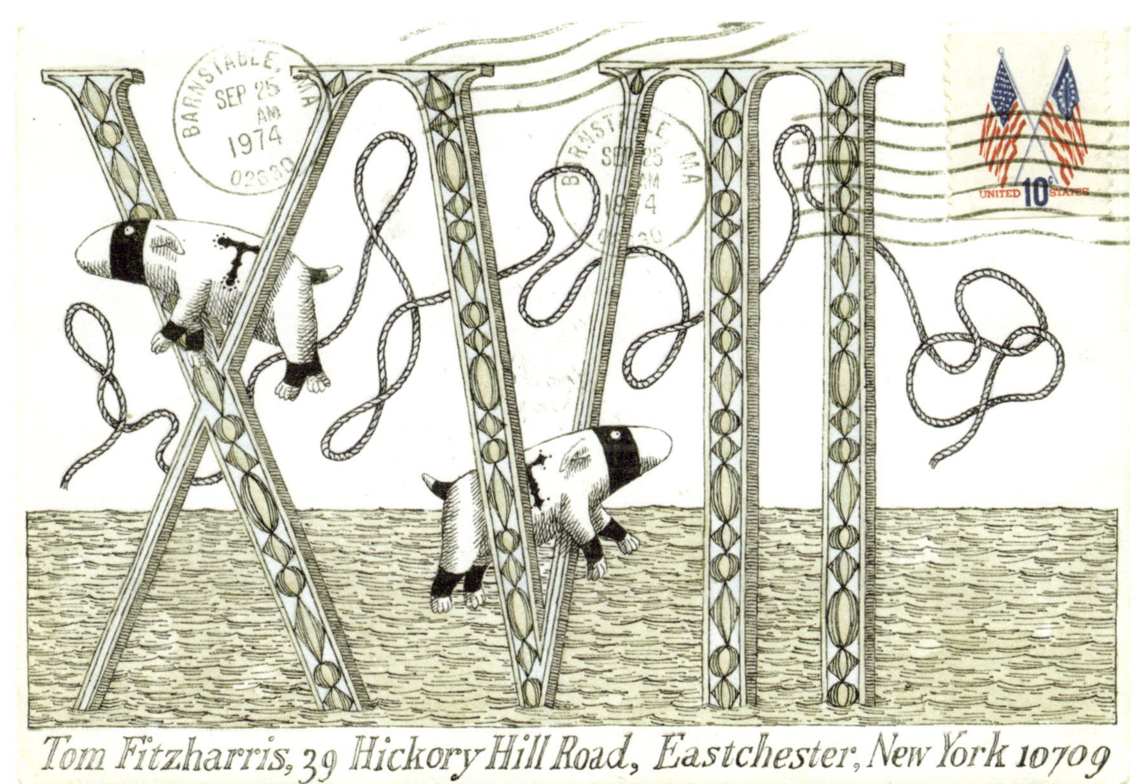

Seventeen

Let reason argue as it will, the heart—
Unlettered, but enlightened—is content
To memorise this visual poetry.

R. H. GRENVILLE, *Horses in the Snow*

HYANNIS, MA
1974
UNITED 10c STATES
TOM
FITZ-
HAR-
RIS
39
Hick-
ory
Hill
Road
East-
chest-
er,
N.Y.
10709
XVIII

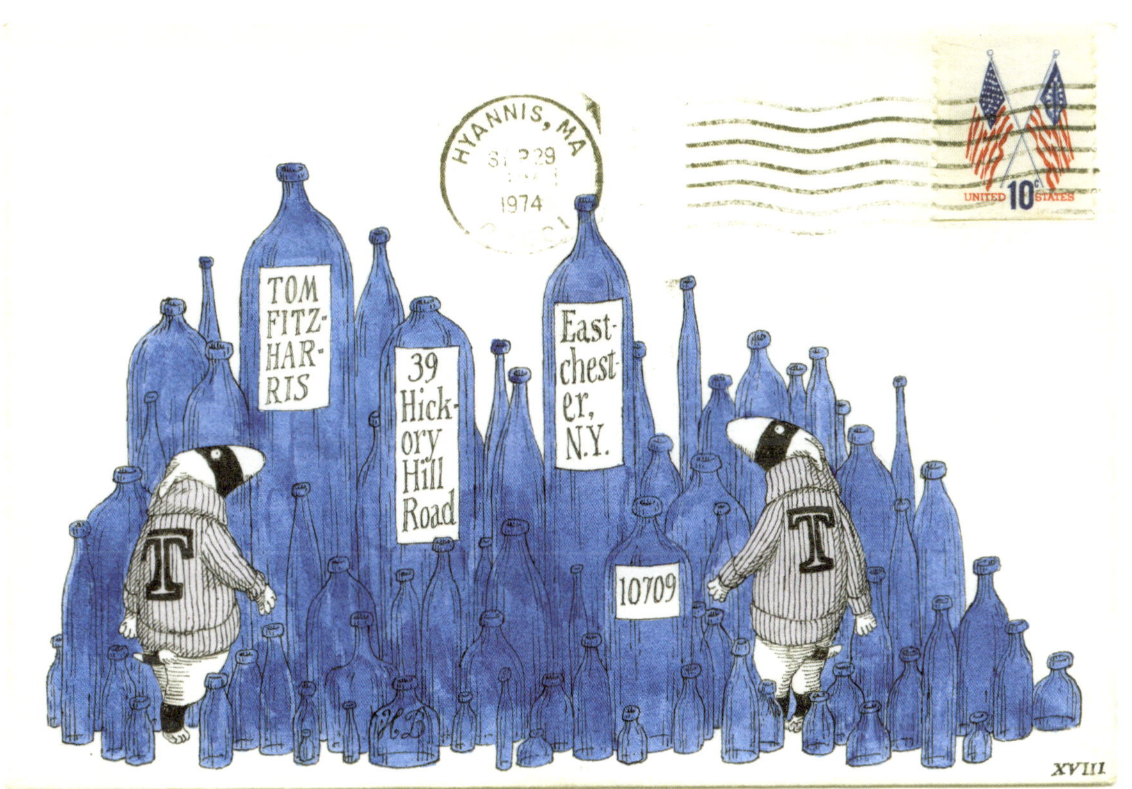

Eighteen

← MESS, NOT MYSTERY

When I look into the fish-ponds in my garden,
Methinks I see a thing arm'd with a rake,
That seems to strike at me.

The Duchess of Malfi, IV. v. 5

Sunday morning, 29.ix.74

I do not think I am going to lose my hand, although it is still stiff and swollen, but now usable, which it wasn't very yesterday.

All the blue bottles are a recollection of a window full of them in one of the antique shops I stopped in after you left that Sunday. The sun coming through them is not reproducible, at least by me.

This is obviously turning out to be a duller-than-ditch/dish-(I have never really known which it is supposed to be)-water communication.

I used to maintain that if it couldn't be put into words it didn't exist; if anything, I believe rather the opposite now. All of which is rather a strangled attempt to say that I appreciated your letter of the 23rd very much, but that I don't know how to say so directly. Yes.

It is very wet and grey, like the inside of my head.

TOM FITZHARRIS
39 Hickory Hill Road
Eastchester, N.Y.
10709
SEP 28
MA
1974
UNITED 10¢ STATES
XIX

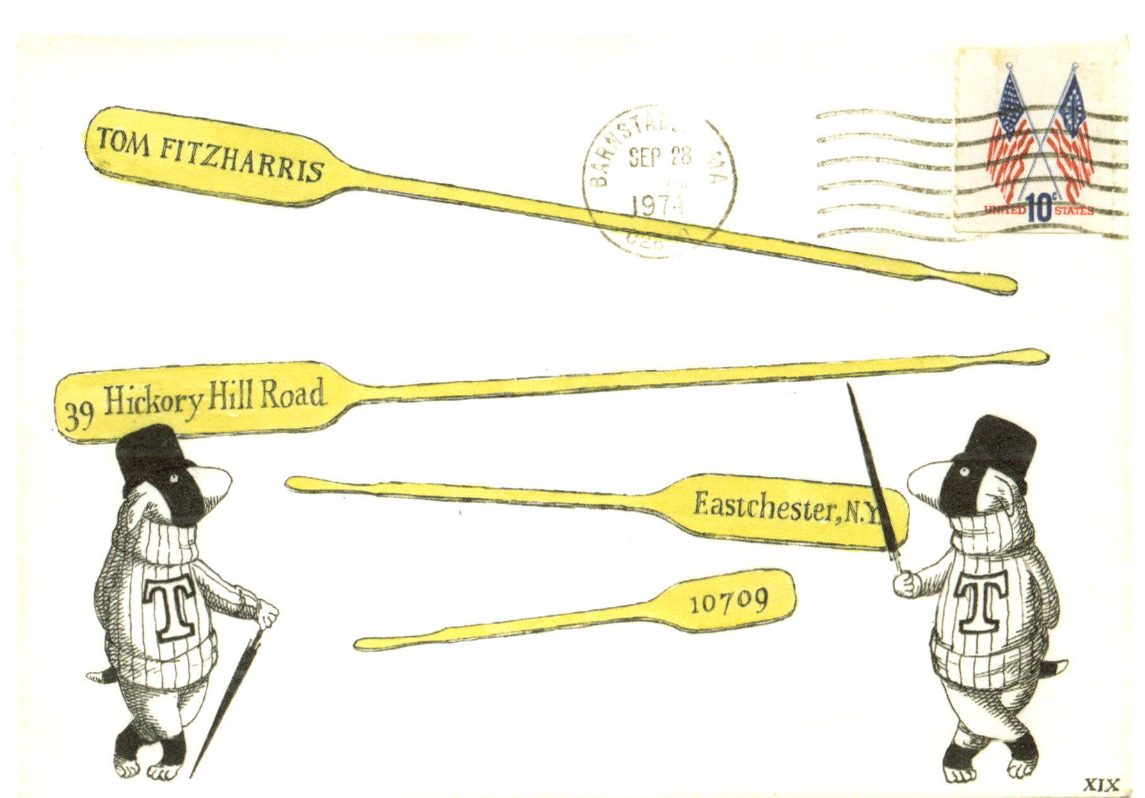

Nineteen

O passer-by, beware!
Is the day fair?
Yet unto evening shall the day spin on
And soon thy sun be gone;
Then darkness come,
And this, a narrow home.

Friday morning, 27.ix.74

What is this have a ~~good~~ nice day jazz? Indeed.

The letter you thought would arrive first did arrive first because the other one isn't here yet.

Sandys Wason (probably) (rather than is) was an eccentric English clergyman who wrote (hopelessly unattainable) light verse, a novel called, if I recollect, Palefox, about which all I know is that it is always snowing in it (v. The Unstrung Harp), and the only book I have of his, an anthology of prefaces and introductions he compiled with someone else.

Proust.

Excerptable dictum:

It is I suppose comprehensible that the letters which we receive from a person are more or less similar and combine to trace an image of the writer so different from the person whom we know as to constitute a second personality. (The Captive, p.48)

Moot, I think.

If you are growing bored with dogs, c'est dommage. We truly creative people never know what is coming next. The wind bloweth where it listeth. Or doesn't of course, from time to time.

Noonish

Oh, crumbs.

I no sooner finished the first drawing for the GB than I discovered it was at variance with the text, and will have to be done all over again.

Seven-thirtyish

Life's little excitements. I was coming upstairs after tea with a notebook for coping with the Fitz-harris Envelope material when Kanzuke got out and confronted one of Betty's cats in the living room. Absolutely stupid me tried to pick him up and in the result he did his best to take off my hand, mostly with his teeth. Blood spurted all over the place, my wrist swelled up like a balloon, almost literally, and it was off to the doctor for a tetanus shot. I can type but just, and I can only hope my hand won't have stiffened up past the drawing point on the mor-row.

TOM FITZHARRIS

39 HICKORY HILL ROAD

EASTCHESTER NEW YORK 10709

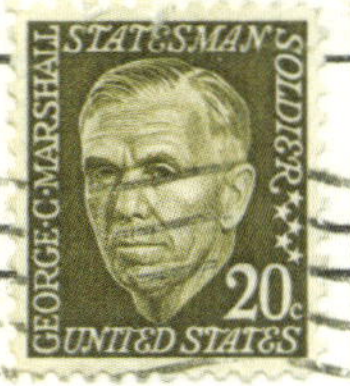

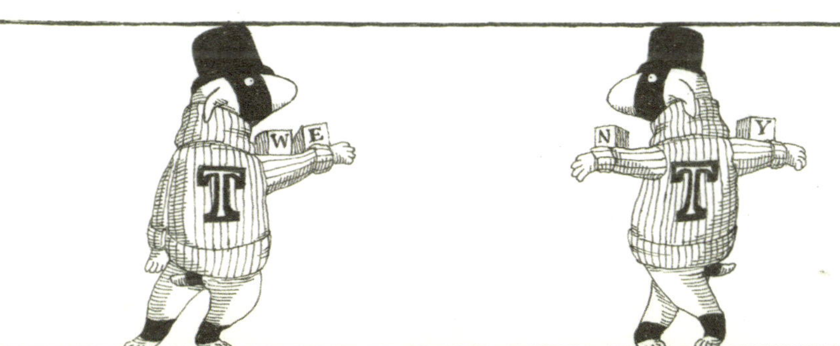

Tom Fitzharris, 39 Hickory Hill Road, Eastchester, N.Y. 10709

Twenty

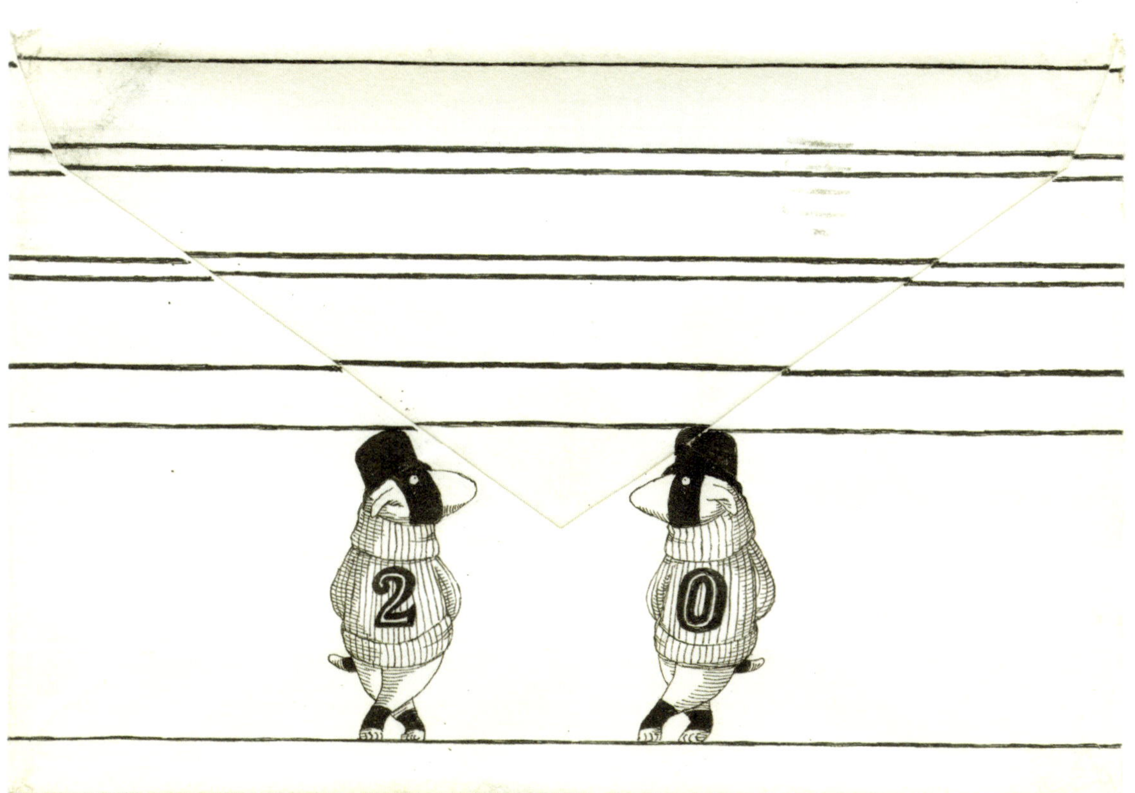
2
0

'Heigh-ho!' cried Fanny; 'was ever such a tiresome carpet as this? It is quite impossible one should ever see anything that is dropt upon it.'

A Visit to the Sea-Side

The true work of art is the one that says less.

CAMUS, *Carnets 1937–1939*

Les souvenirs sont cors de chasse
Dont meurt la bruit parmi le vent

APOLLINAIRE

Monday morning, 30.ix.74

The typed address is removable, if you wish. After I had settled on the lettering and it was too late, I realized its legibility was doubtful.

As to postmarks, look at it this way. They add a Proustian dimension of time.

I was certainly being more something (dreary) than usual in my last, at least I hope so, if you follow. Anyway, Never apologize, never explain, which is what I am always doing nothing else but.

If ever you get a letter from me all handwritten, cursive or otherwise, you will know I have gone round the bend.

I'll include the Apollinaire quote on a card in this.

In the meantime time and cats are combining to reduce the attic to a shambles in one way or another. Using that pile of cranberry crates as a launching pad they are gradually managing to bring down one item after another from the rafters. The latest casuality was the hay rake, if that's what it is, and everything attached to it. Also the furniture is all coming apart at the joints... There was a rain of frogs every few minutes for a while there, so they are all tucked away in a small wooden trunk-like affair.

And so another week is in train. What a creepy thought.

Do you want to sit around here, or take off for remote parts of New England when next you come up?

We hold these Truths...
UNITED STATES 10c
OCT 4
AM
39
Hickory Hill Road
TOM FITZHARRIS
10709
Eastchester New York

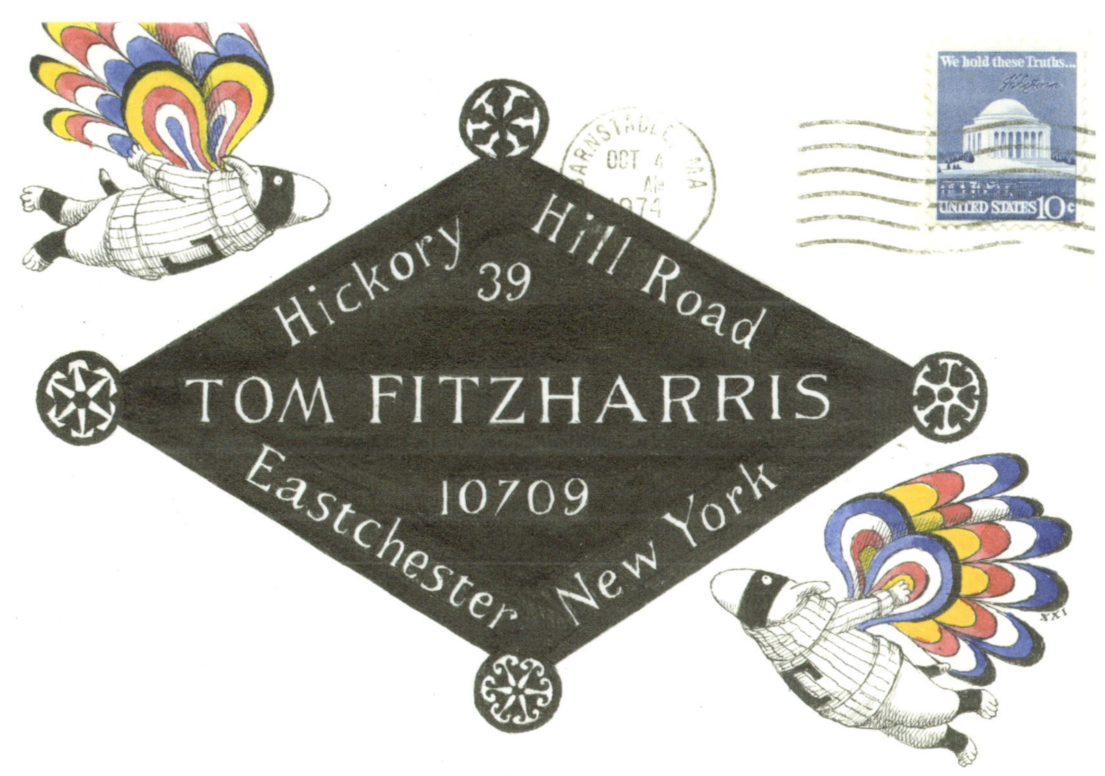

Twenty-One

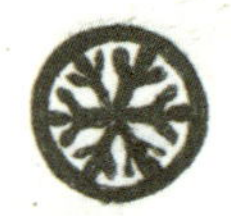

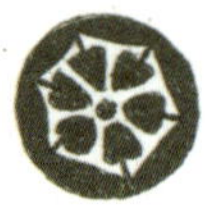

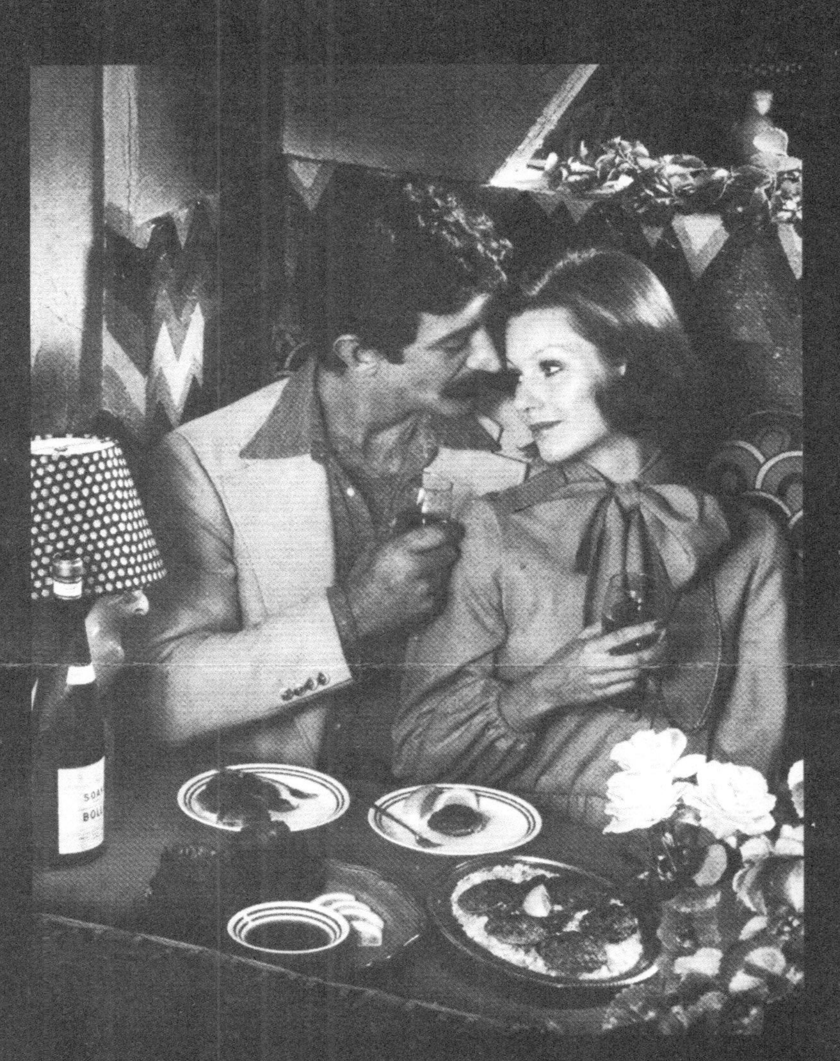

BAKED CLAMS AL COMO •
MARINATED ARTICHOKES • SOAVE BOLLA 1971.
JUST THE BEGINNING—AT COMO INN,
546 MILWAUKEE AVENUE, CHICAGO.
FOR RESERVATIONS 421-5222
FREE PARKING.

The world is a place of such uncertainty and change that what we imagine we see before our eyes really does not exist and what has a beginning is likely to be without end.

KENKO, *Essays in Idleness*

Friday morning, 4.x.74

I finished The Past Recaptured at breakfast this morning. I'm now going to read the two volume biography by Painter and Proust's Binoculars, which I found in a battered paperback copy in Parnassus yesterday. Then we shall see.

Your letters of the 30th and the 1st both arrived this morning, along with a plethora of this and that, most of it all too tedious, involving nasty little retorts to my bank, my dentist's bill-keeper, and the like. Which is what I've been doing.

The enclosed ad shows that Chicago is trying but is also a trifle confused.

I just sent off the second version of the first drawing of The Green Beads to Soho. I hope to get the whole thing done by the time you arrive.

o
H.B. stands for Heure Bleue (not Hector Blitho).

We hold these Truths...
UNITED STATES 10c
TOM
FITZHARRIS
39
Hickory
Hill
Road
Eastchester
New
York
10709
XXII

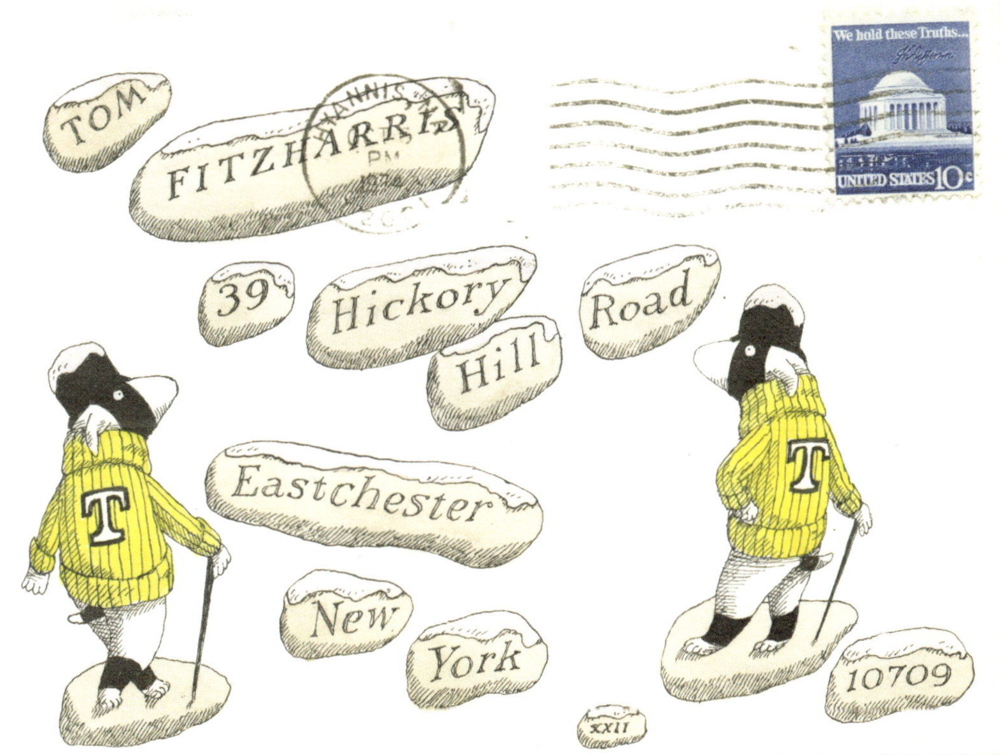

Twenty-Two

It is the intangibility of the distinction
that gives it its point.

I. COMPTON-BURNETT

Saturday morning, 5.x.74

I enclose a rehearsal pass for yours or someone else's possible use. (I contributed an inordinate amount to the Ballet Guild a short time ago.)

The Apollinaire is called Cors de chasse.

In verifying same I came across the last quatrain of Cortege, which I cannot resist. (The translation is Shattuck's.)

Rien n'est mort que ce qui n'existe pas encore
Près du passé luisant demain est incolore
Il est informe aussi près de ce qui parfait
Présente tout ensemble et l'effort et l'effet

Nothing is dead but what has never been
The colored past outshines tomorrow's grey
Besides whose formlessness it can display
The sequence of the effort and effect

If I have sent you this before you can always paste this one over the bathroom mirror.

Don't bother bringing the envelopes, but thank you anyway. I have remembered as much as necessary about the ones I was somewhat vague on. In any case it is only that I don't want to repeat myself more than is absolutely necessary.

New Hampshire is of course feasible, but as you always say, Tom, although I never happen to have heard you actually do so, let's play it by ear. And hope that one or both of us is not struck with instant deafness at some awkward moment. Such as being stalled on the tracks as the express roars into view.

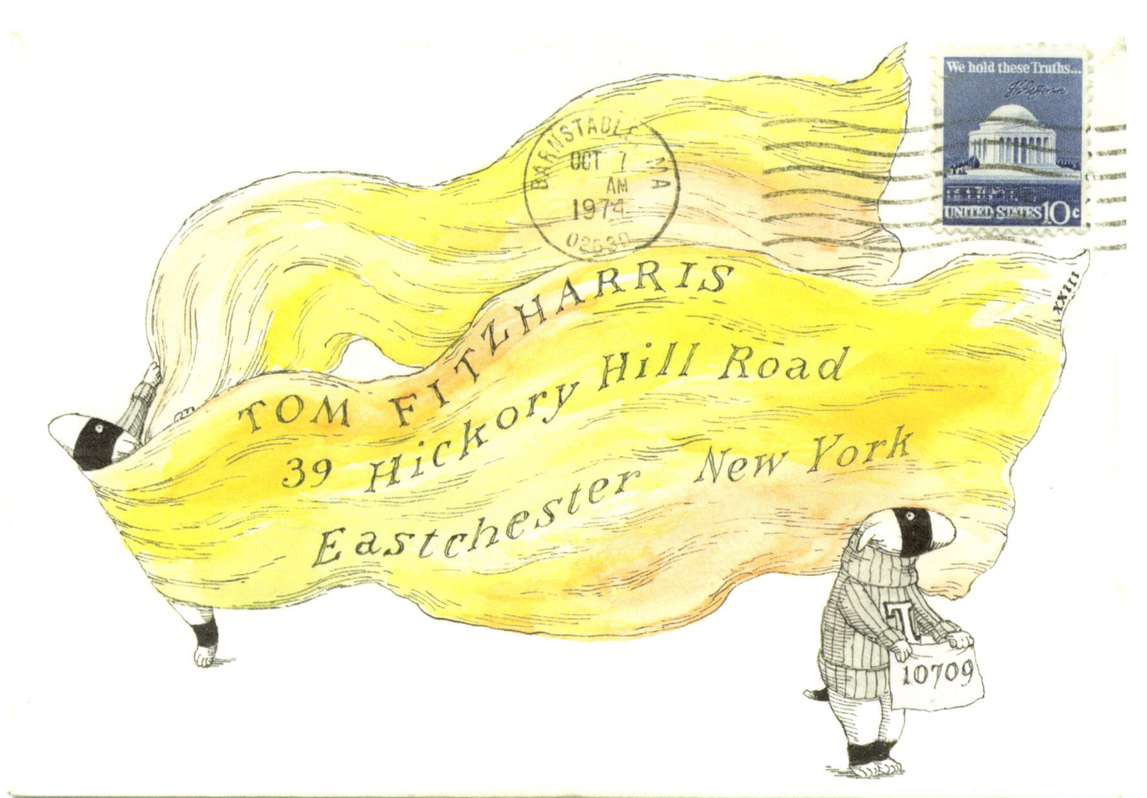

Twenty-Three

Nothing real is simple.

AMIEL

Only that which changes remains true.

JUNG

We hold these Truths...
UNITED STATES 10c
OCT 12
AM
MA
1974
02630
Tom Fitzharris, 39 Hickory Hill Road, Eastchester, New York 10709
XXIV

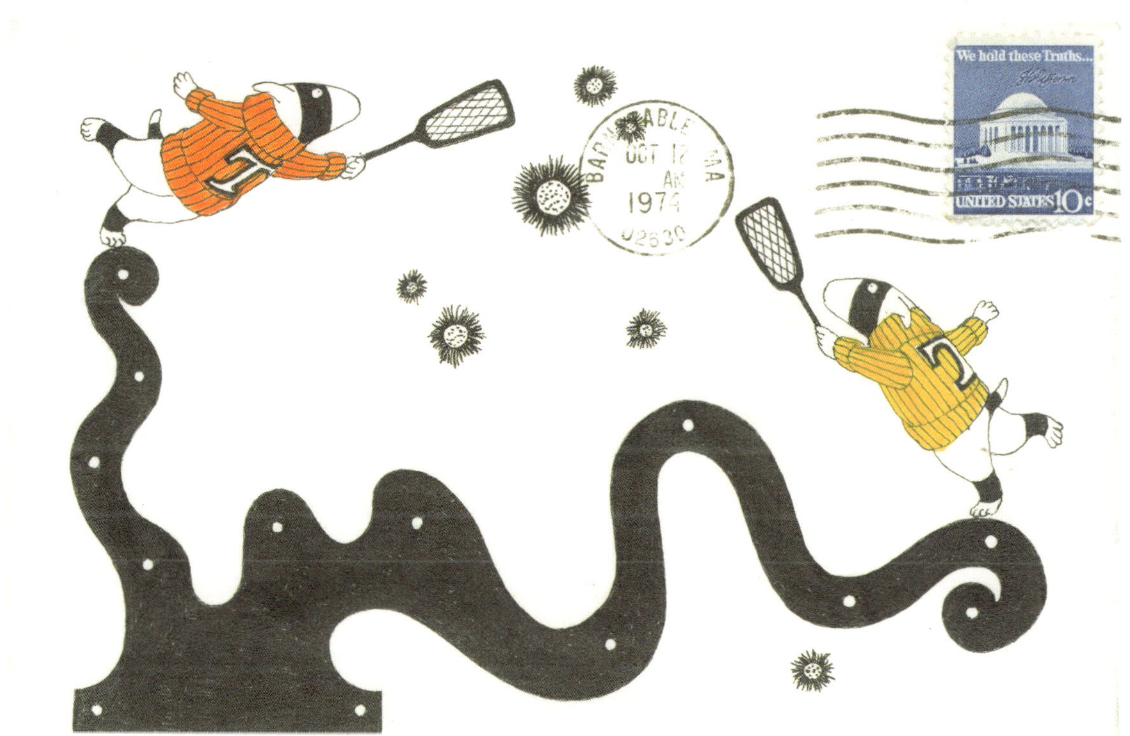

Twenty-Four

Nothing is made of nought, of all things made,
Their abstract being a dream but of a shade.

GEORGE CHAPMAN, *Bussy D'Ambois*, V.iv.

Saturday morning, 12.x.74

The mails are really inexplicable. Your letter of the 8th just got here. It proves you are not only witty, which of course I knew, else why would I bother talking to you, but that you have a very contemporary vocabulary (and outlook). Like wow!

I don't have Agatha Christie's address except on the letter on my wall, but your sister could always write her in care of Dodd, Mead.

The last envelope was not meant as any direct reference to your dancing, which I have never seen.

Do you think the enclosed quote means anything, and if so, what? or do you suppose I copied it down wrong in the long, long ago?

I think I'd better hasten this into the mails, or else you will get it after you have been here.

In the meantime, as Mr Kirstein said his mother used to tell him, Don't create in front of the servants.

Or, as the song says, Life is a rock, but the radio rolls me.

TOM FITZHARRIS
39 Hickory Hill Road
Eastchester
New York 10709
We hold these Truths...
UNITED STATES 10c
25
T
T

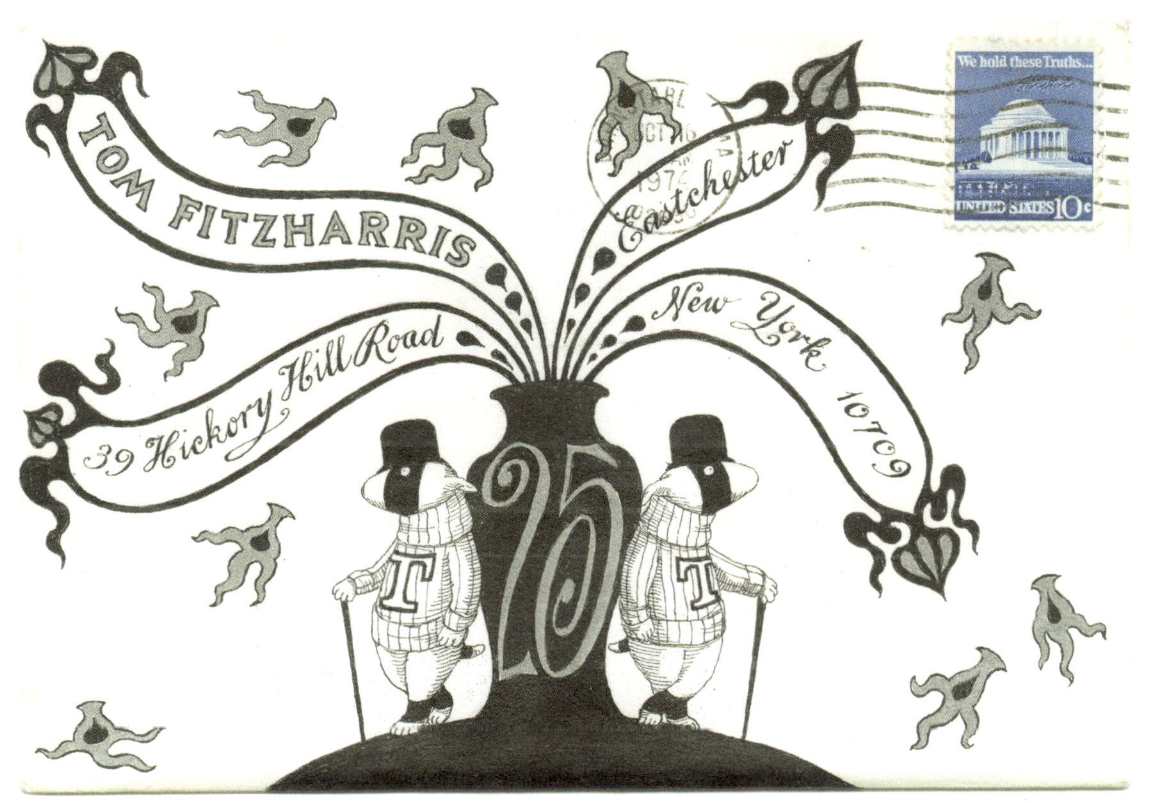

Twenty-Five

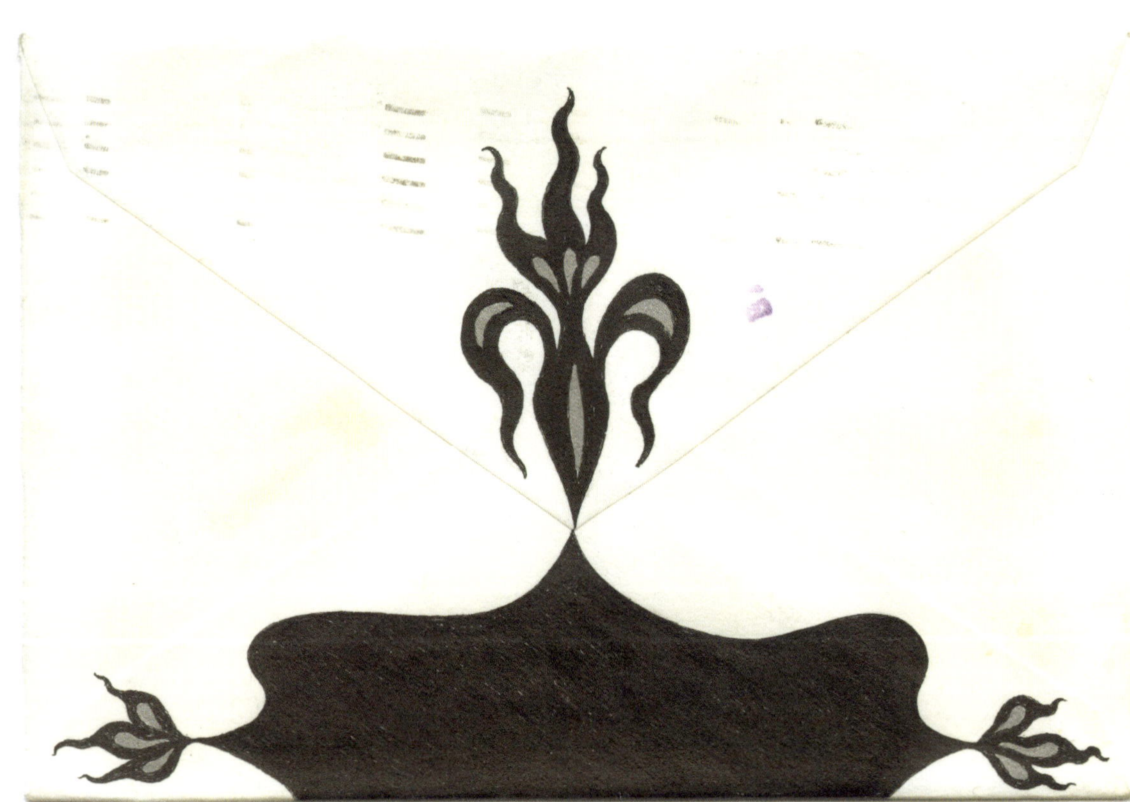

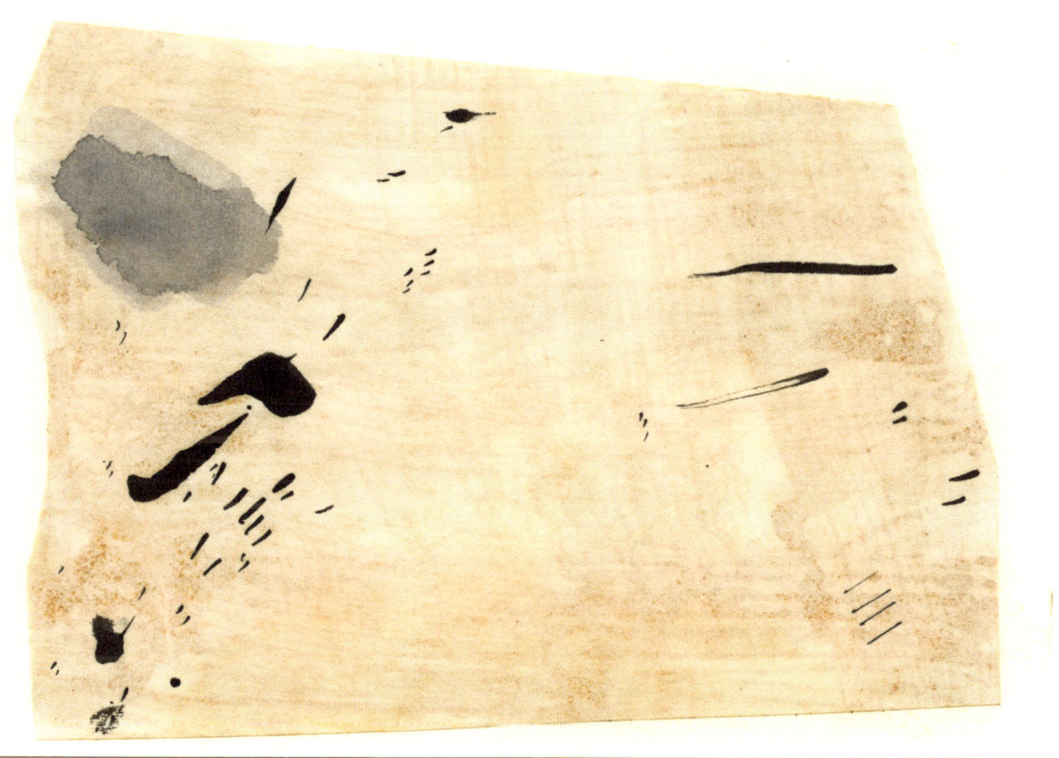

Inadvertent drawing (ink and water colour) 14-16.x.74

Whatever we see when awake is death;
when asleep, dreams.

HERACLITUS

Tom Fitzharris,
39 Hickory Hill
Road, Eastchester,
New York 10709
We hold these Truths...
UNITED STATES 10c
26

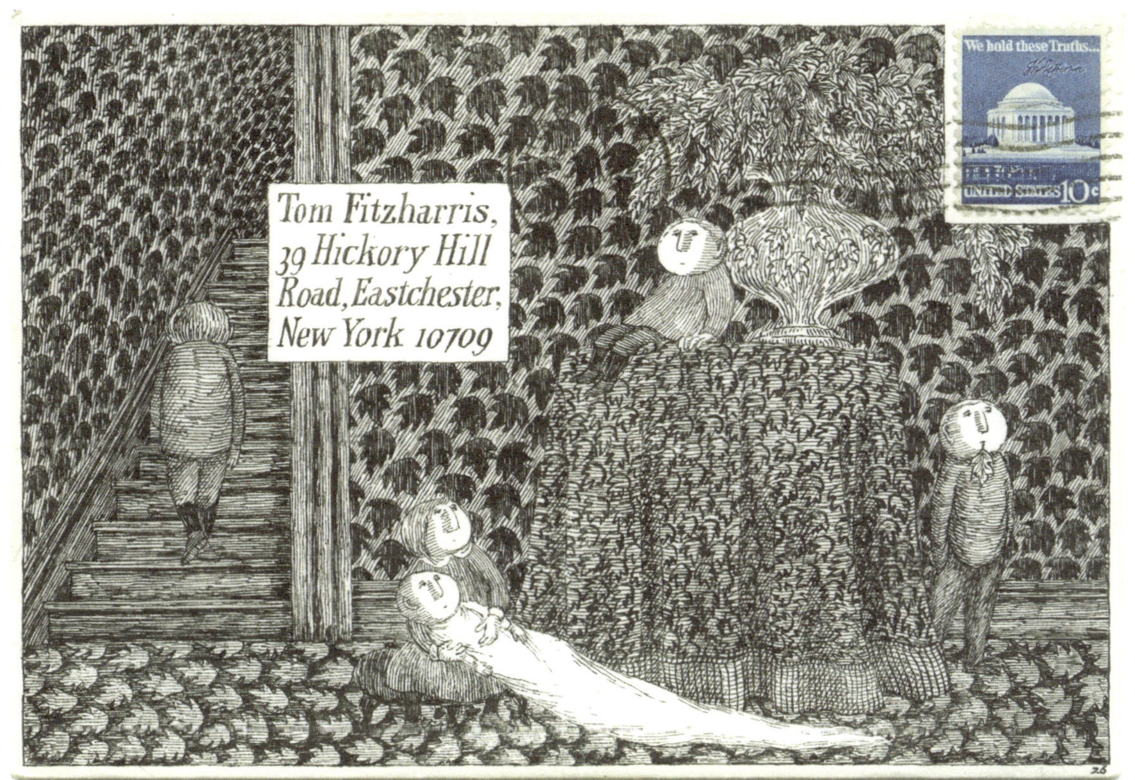

Twenty-Six

There was a brief snow squall out the window just as I got up, and I was overcome by a feeling of 'winter coming down, winter closing in'

Monday morning, 21.x.74

I can usually count on post-house-guest-depression to be alleviated, no matter how pleasant it has been to have them here, by a certain part of me thinking, 'Thank God they've gone, and I can get back to puttering around all by myself.' Alas, I discover this is not always to be relied on. Well.

I trust you had an uneventful drive back and were in time for the telly.

Monday evening

If you ever wish (and I can't imagine that you won't) ~~wish~~ to use the bathroom in a private house, the correct thing to say is, in as diffi~~c~~dent a voice as possible, 'May I take advantage of your hospitality?' I have this on the authority of my aunt Isabel who was over to help finish up leftovers this evening, and she got it from two elderly ladies of the family's acquaintance, actually one of them having been vaguely related, who during World War I approached my grndfather and asked him if he would take them under his protection when, as they believed was about to happen, German submarines appeared in Lake Michigan. (I should have mentioned this all took place in Chicago.)

Tuesday morning

My car is off being aligned front and rear. I took yet another shower~~e~~ this morning; I hope all this water won't make my skin peel off or something. I am racing through V. To the envelope.

Afternoon

I must say I find this envelope rather baffling.

No quote on a card because I have already pasted the stamp on the envelope some time ago, and I'm afraid the quote might make for Postage Due and somehow they would never even give you the opporti unity to pay and have the ~~nevlope~~ envelope publicly burned in New Jersey. Or something.

I have a dreadful apprehension that I am going to be reduced to seeing Class of '42 and Summer of '42 towards the end of the week. Au secours. I still have to do the stairs and the perspective wallpaper which at the ~~mmmmxxx~~ moment I don't see how I am going to do....

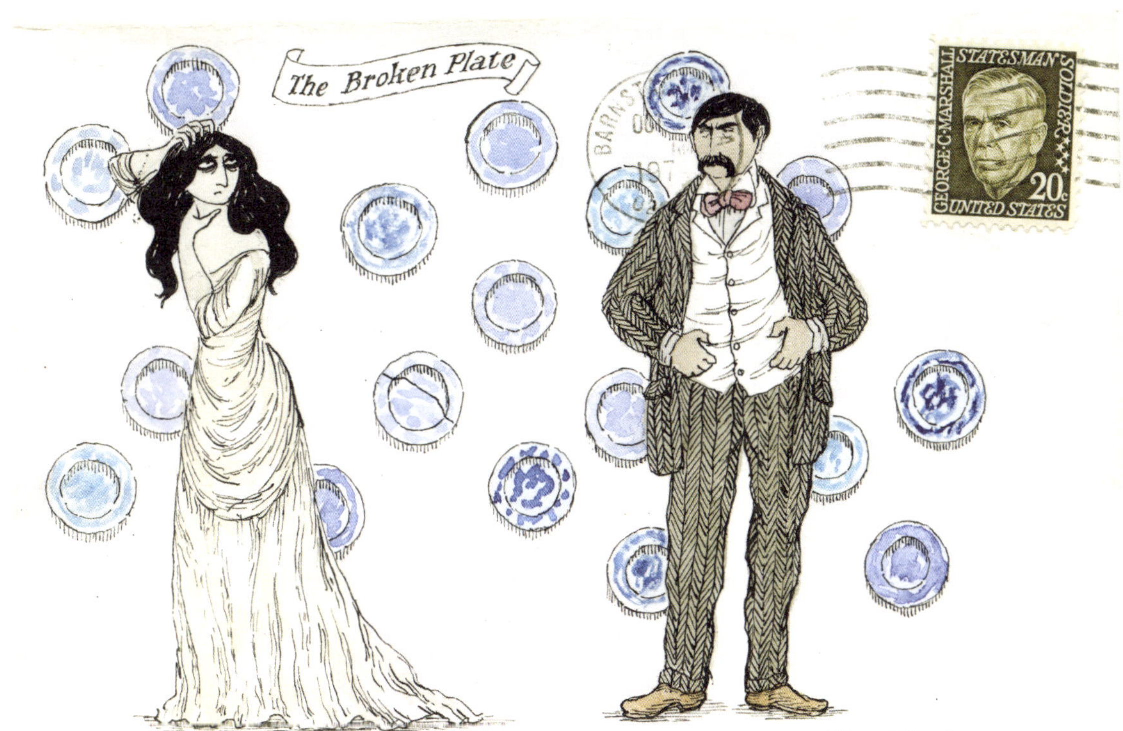

Twenty-Seven

Perdu: l'expression même est comme une cloche

KEATS, *trans.* HUGH KENNER

Monday morning, very early

The phone rang Friday night at about 12:30 while I was dreaming that Miss Steloff was telling me something very interesting about the way Gertrude Stein wrote, but by the time I had lurched down the attic stairs in the dark and got to the phone it had stopped ringing. So begins chapter several thousand and something of Les Ennuis de la vie quotidienne.

Connie came over on the 10 o'clock boat from the Vineyard Saturday morning, and will stay until tomorrow, but otherwise this holiday weekend is giving an unnerving impression of Things Going Wrong.

I suspected I might not hear from you last week, but it was still discouraging not to. My aunt Isabel misunderstood my perfectly clear invitation for dinner Saturday night, and by the time we wondered where she was and called, she had already eaten.

The cats are behaving abominably to each other.

The weather, not partaking of the general whatsit, has been beautiful, so we've been driving about a lot, including Provincetown yesterday afternoon, which was packed with lots of unattractive people, and the marine surplus store which is usually filled with all sorts of amusing things to buy was this time definitely not.

Oh yes, and also Saturday night just as we were starting to cook dinner after Isabel had been communicated with, somebody I hadn't heard from all summer asked us over for an early (it was now close to seven and we were already half-plotze)

drink, though not dinner because they were going out somewhere else, and that was all very strange because somebody I was sure would be there wasn't, and somebody I was sure wouldn't be, was, and there were also several dotty ladies from Nantucket, one of whom incidentally told me that somebody had bought the Dracula set(s) for their very bright fourteen year old son, and that it was now in a New York apartment, a rather large one I must assume.

Then of course neither of us remembered about daylight saving going out so there we were temporally at sea all of yesterday.

Not to mention that fundamentally I am now beginning to come unstuck, unglued, and unhinged by Impending Change from Cape to NY.

In the meantime Connie and I have been reviewing our collective past, which goes back over thirty-five years, and are struck once again (surprise!) by the Utter Inconsequence of It All.

How I detest holidays.

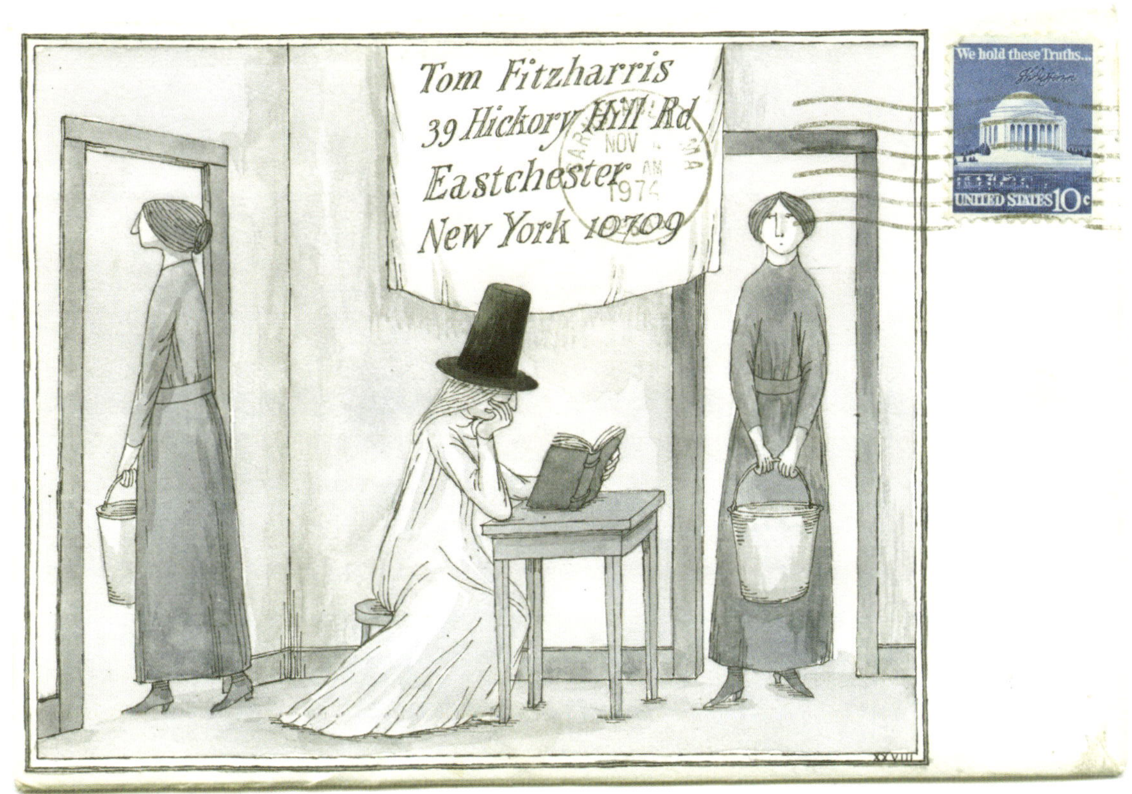

Twenty-Eight

Toujours les tripes.

EZRA POUND

Thursday morning, 31.x.74

I went off to Charlestown, Marblehead, Nahant, etc. yesterday, met seven cats, a bulldog, assorted flighty types, and both of Mr Marshall's friends, although not at the same time, and got home around midnight. It was all really very pleasant, and in the result I couldn't be more depressed. So tomorrow it's off to Mt Holyoke, but I hope I can manage to get back rather earlier; that I expect will nevertheless be also depressing. It must be me.

The Heraclitus quote comes from _Heraclitus_ by Philip Wheelwright, an Athenaeum paperback. What's yours?

Were you able to exchange the jacket so that you won't turn into Quasimodo? I hope so.

And here we are at the bottom of the page, or almost.

Saturday morning

What else did you expect would happen at work the minute you got involved in moving? Tell yourself all the brouhaha is good for you, especially since it probably isn't at all, and is only driving you up the wall. The one on which the handwriting always is, and always illegible. You can see what state I am in. I do sympathize, and a lot of good that does you.

Also never apologize, never explain; in this case because if you do, it will all become a great drag and you won't want to write. On the other hand, I apologize for the endless ~~pxxk~~ packet you must have received the end of this week.

An impressionable lady in Wales
Had a passion for tragical tales;
   The torrents of tears
   That she wept through the years
They came and collected in pails.

Overcome by an impulse to cook,
A certain young man undertook
   To turn out a stew—
   Made from golf balls and glue—
That he found in a curious book.

Little Jane, who'd read all about bears,
Went to see them asleep in their lairs;
   This was a mistake:
   They were all wide awake,
And dancing the tango in pairs.

(Concocted for a Children's Book Council pamphlet, where I hardly expect they'll appear)

UNITED 10 STATES
Tom Fitzharris, 39 Hickory Hill Road, Eastchester, New York 10709
XXIX

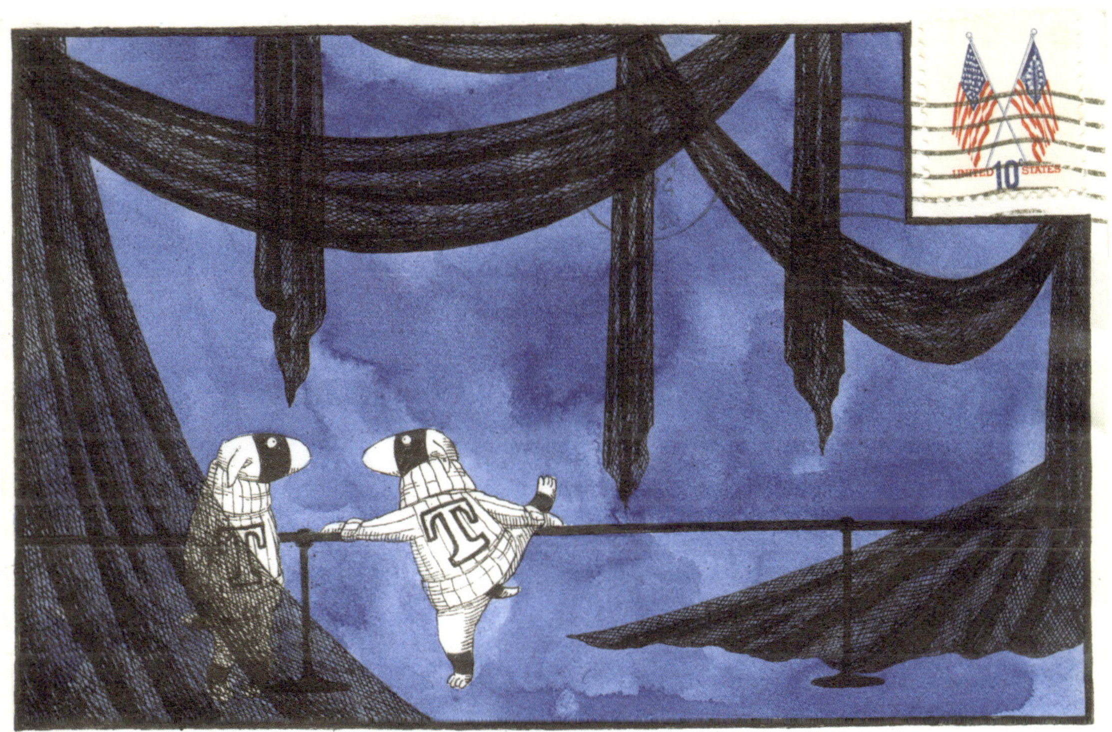

Twenty-Nine

All your anxiety is because of your desire for harmony.
Seek disharmony; then you will gain peace.

JALAL-UD-DIN RUMI, *Persian poet 1207–93*

Monday morning, 4.xi.74

I hope this incident will teach you not to try and have fun with people.

Tuesday night

I was sitting here going into stupefaction, working on the envelope (which is a rejected idea for HB which I couldn't resist executing anyway) and listening to election returns, having done three HB drawings today, and had just risen feeling I could not put another pen line to paper and looked out the window to see a police car in the driveway. There is a sinister fog about and so with my tumbler of Dubonnet in hand I tottered downstairs and outdoors only to find the police car empty, its radio going, its door open. I prudently stood in the headlights, not wishing to be shot be the policeman whenever he returned, which he ultimately did waving a flashlight from the far side of the house. After ascertaining I was Mr Gorey, he said my publisher, whoever that may be, had been trying to get me unsuccessfully by phone and was afraid something had happened to me, and so forth and so on. Really.

Wednesday morning

The refrigerator leaks in the night, the light in the upstairs hall suddenly refuses to turn off, I did a washing that included a full fountain pen....

Later

I can't think why I offered you framed prints. Now that I know you are having bookcases to the ceiling I am going to lend you books: several thousands of them. Please let me know as soon as possible when I can arrange to have them delivered. (What a load off my mind—and my floor.) Just think, you will be able to appear cultivated to even the most casual and ill-informed dropper-in.

As you can gather I am in a vaguely loopy frame of mind.

The enclosed quote I find (for myself at any rate) almost too a propos, but then I tried to decide when I wouldn't, and couldn't, and so forth, and so on...

Later

I trust you are feeling better about things this week and that this will reach you by the end of it. This is all I am trusting at the moment. Actually I am only writing this letter so that you will owe me one in July.

HYANNIS, MA
NOV 10
1974
UNITED STATES
10
ANOTHER WRONG SHADE
YET ANOTHER WRONG SHADE
A WRONG SHADE
TOM FITZHARRIS
39 Hickory Hill Road
Eastchester New York
10709
THIRTY
A WHITE NIGHT

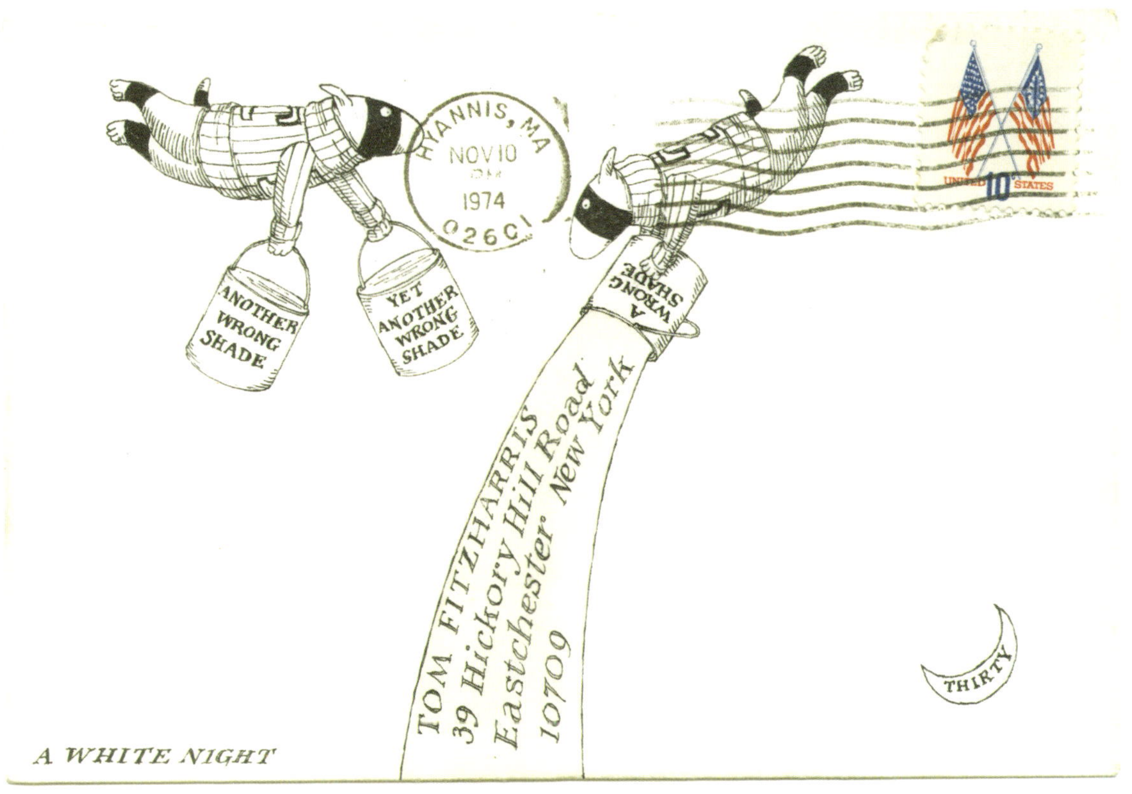

Thirty

Life is too short not to travel first class.

WYNDHAM LEWIS

Tom Fitzharris
76 Bank Street
New York, N.Y.
10014
14 NOV
1974
31

We hold these Truths...
UNITED STATES 10c

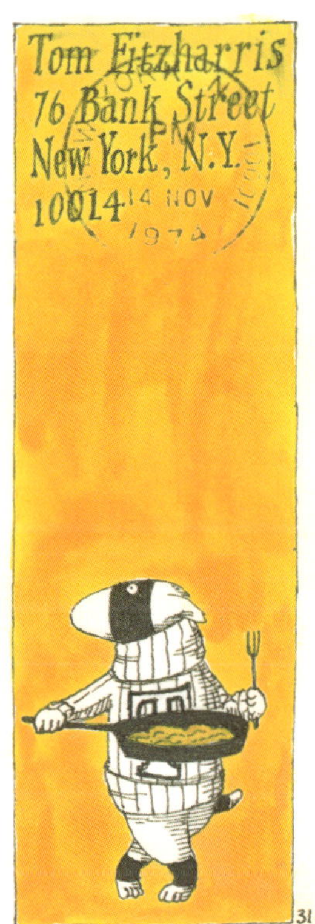

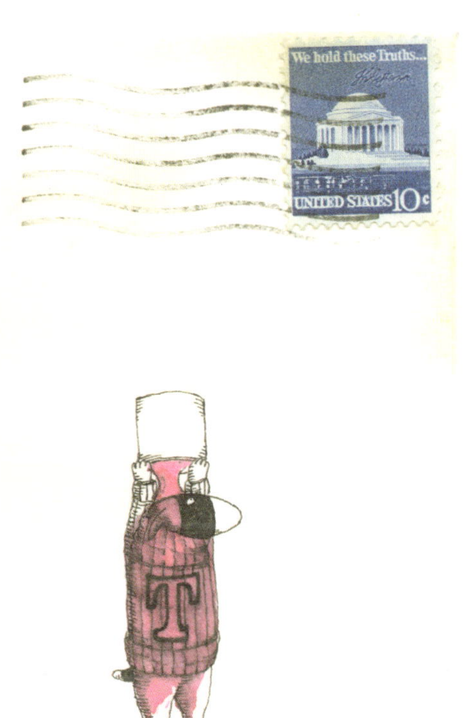

Thirty-One

. . . it is appalling that some of Edward Gorey's more radical tales sneaked out through publishing's side door.

RICHARD KOSTELANETZ, *The End of Intelligent Writing*

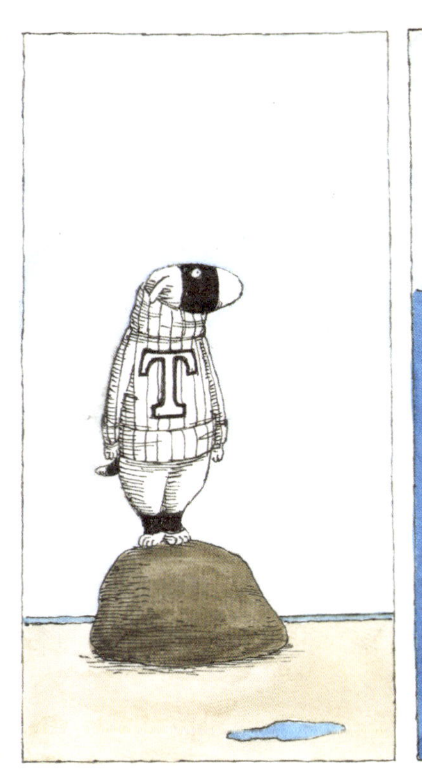

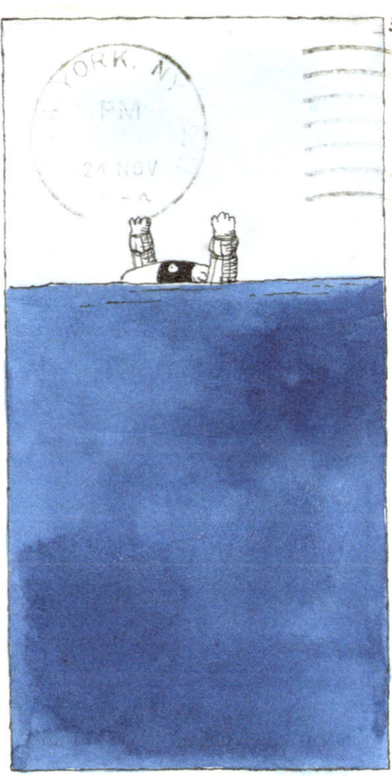

32

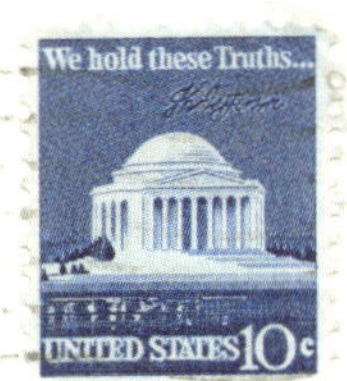

Tom Fitzharris,
76 Bank Street,
New York, N.Y. 10014

Thirty-Two

32

Twice a day I am quite suicidal,
Yet twice I am shrieking with glee:
Why must Life be so dreadfully tidal?
O get me away from the *sea*!

From the German of EDUARD BLUTIG

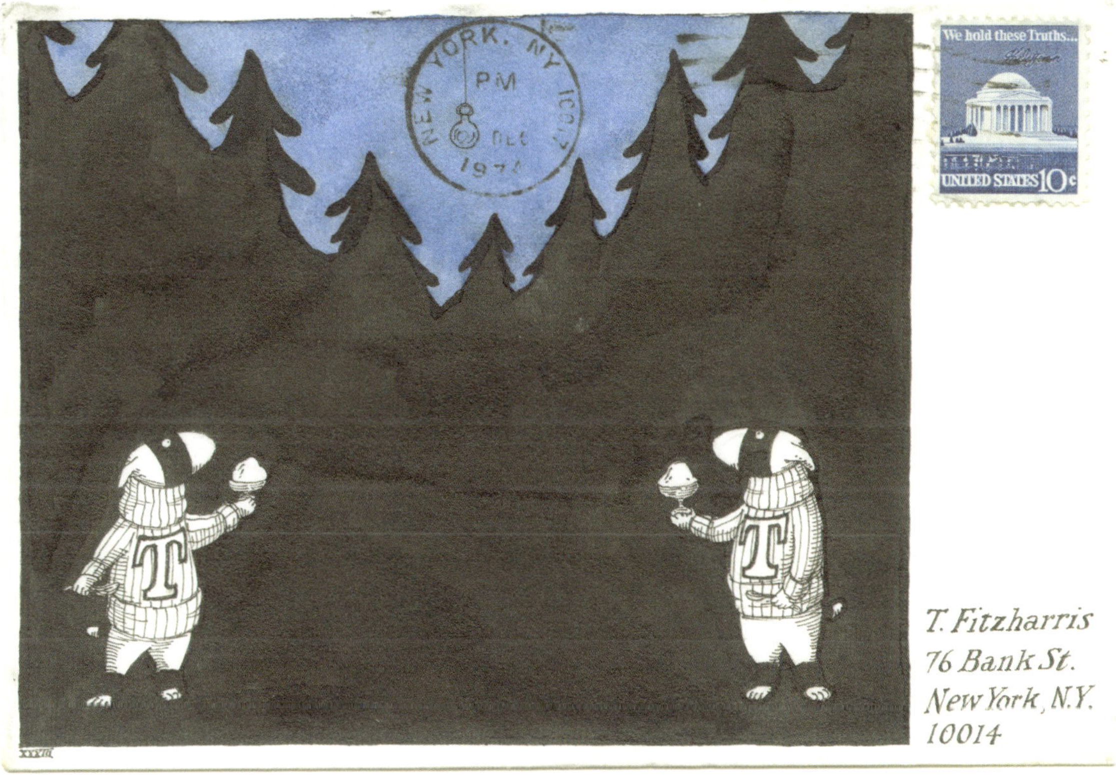

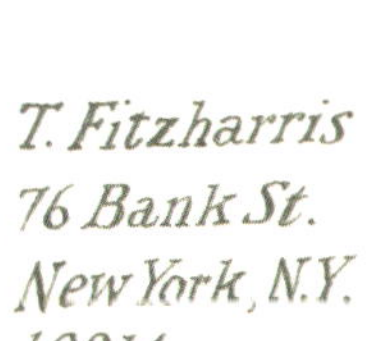

Thirty-Three

Let be be finale of seem.
The *only emperor* is the emperor of ice-cream.

WALLACE STEVENS

UNITED 10¢ STATES
I'm very good at picking up stones.
XXXIV
Tom Fitzharris, 76 Bank Street, New York, N.Y. 10014

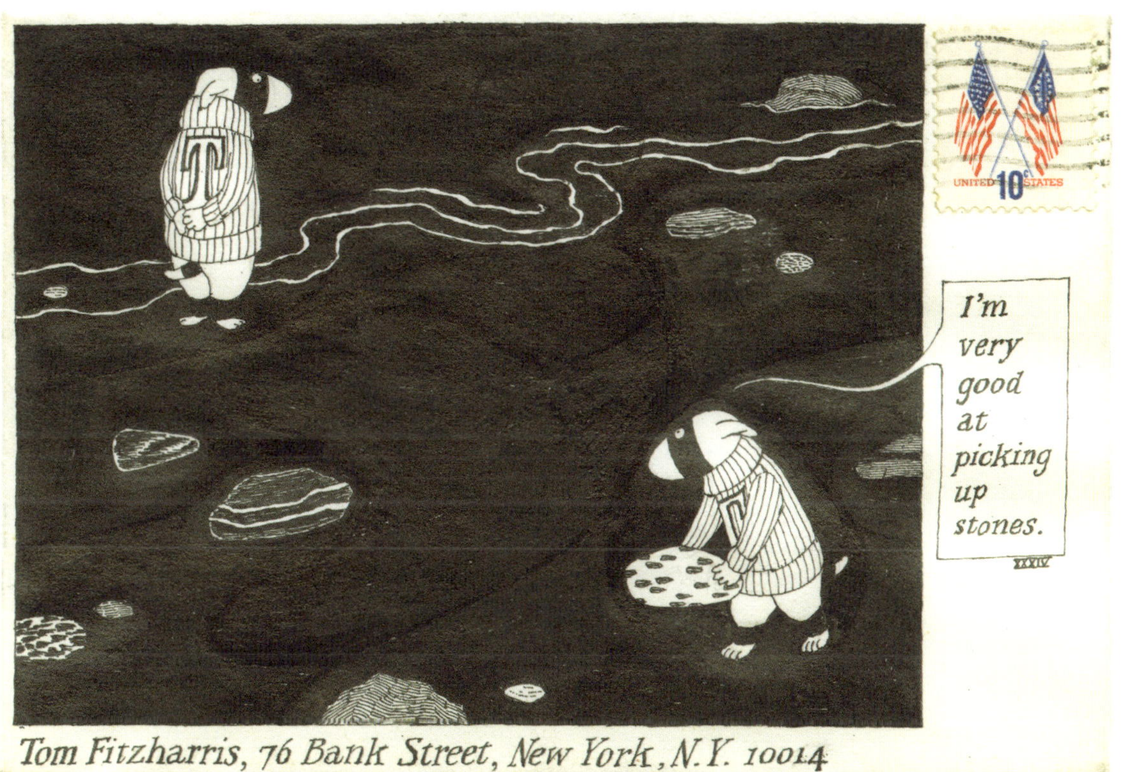

Thirty-Four

Our own journey is entirely imaginative.
Therein lies its strength.

CÉLINE

We hold these Truths...
UNITED STATES 10c
35. Un avant-goût d'un ouvrage futur
Les Passementeries horribles
Tom Fitzharris, 76 Bank Street, New York, N.Y. 10014

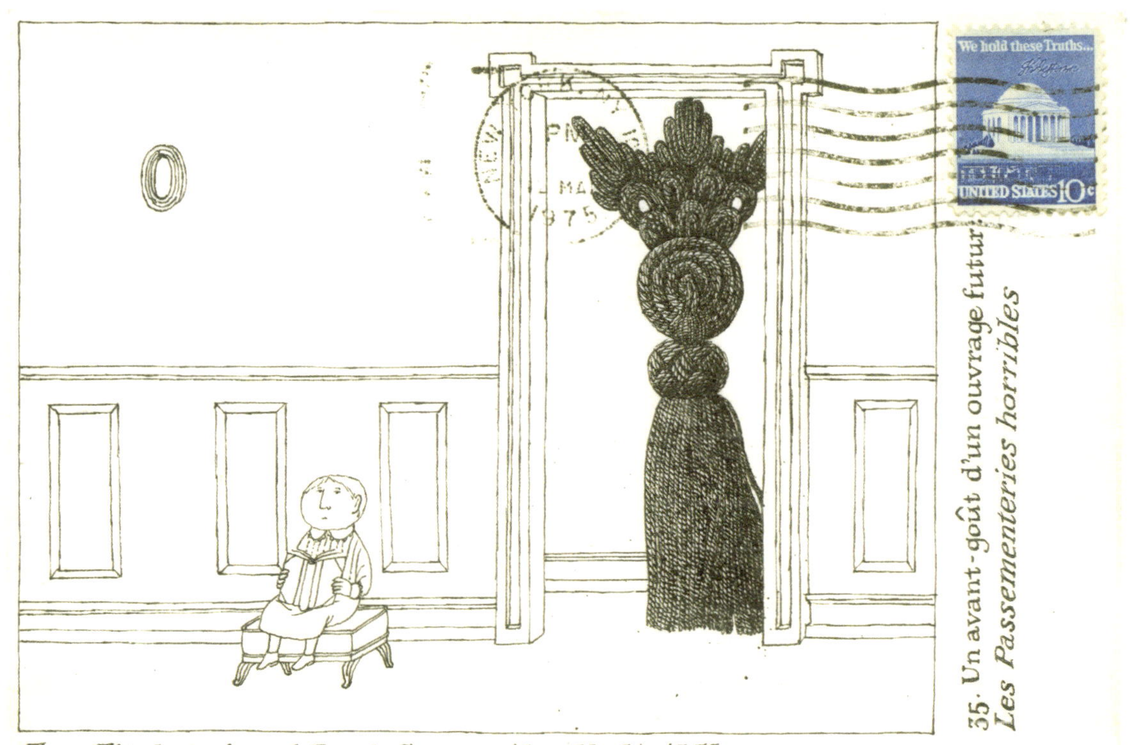

Thirty-Five

Inspiration is the moment when one knows what is happening. In general, we do not know what is happening.

MAGRITTE

We hold these Truths...
UNITED STATES 10c
Tom Fitzharris
76 Bank Street
New York, N.Y. 10014
XXXVI

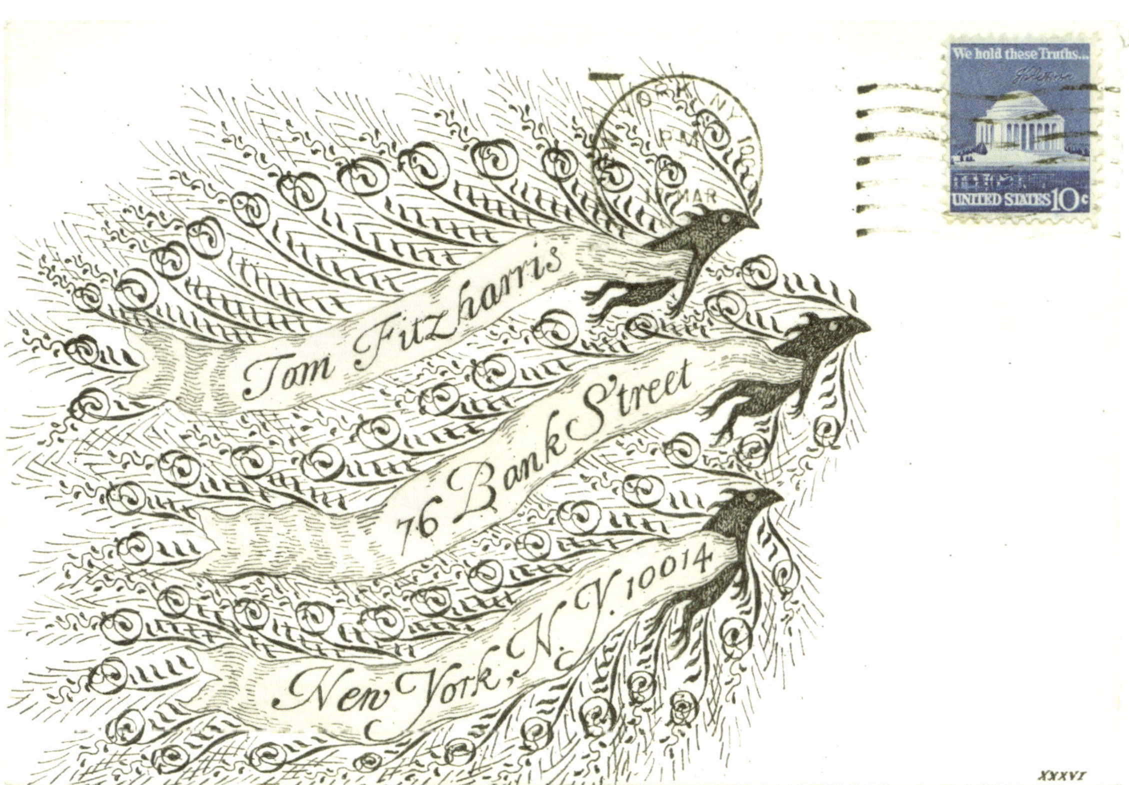

Thirty-Six

I've always thought of friendship as where two people really tear one another apart and perhaps in that way learn something from one another.

FRANCIS BACON

Thirty-Seven

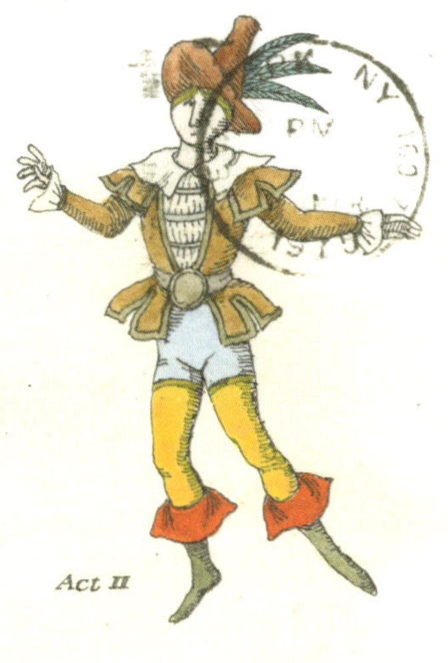

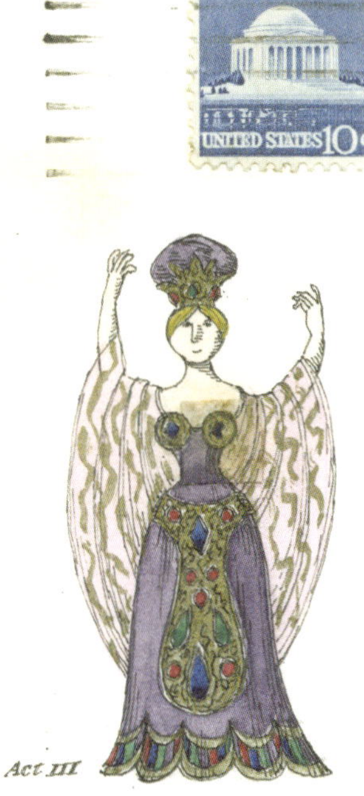

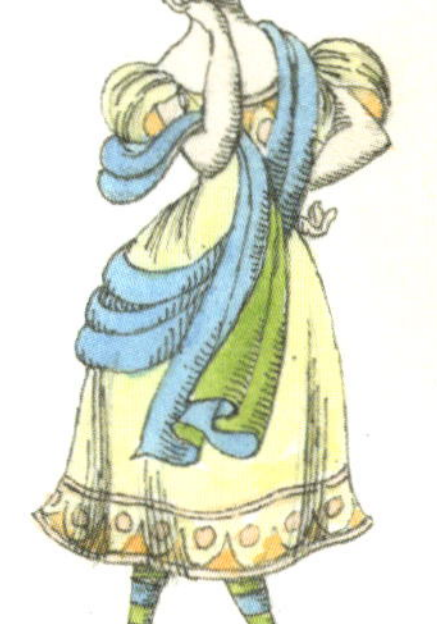

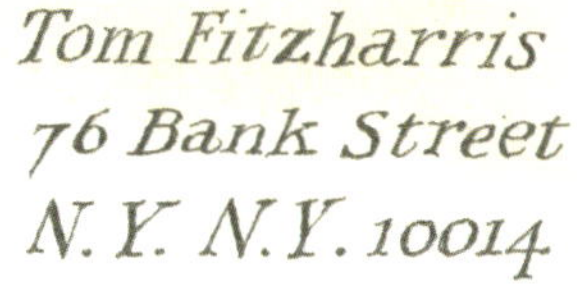

(37)

L'amour que l'on nous vante comme la cause de nos plaisirs, n'en est au plus que le prétexte.

Les Liaisons Dangereuses

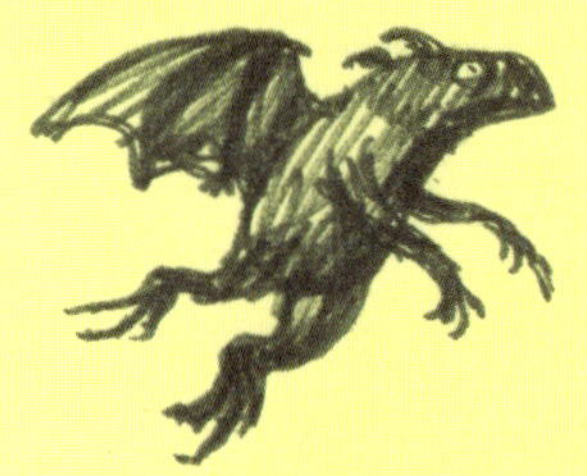

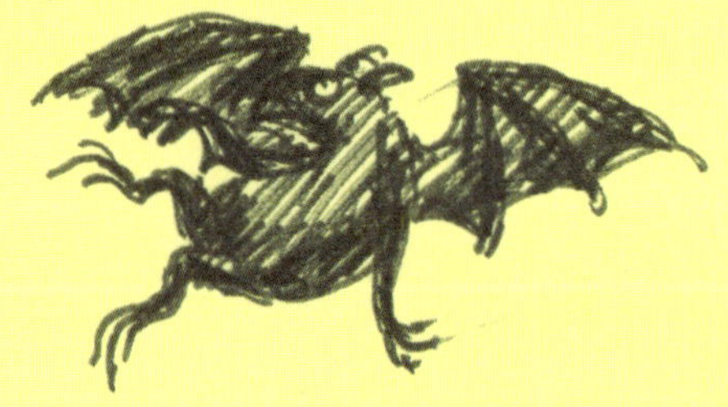

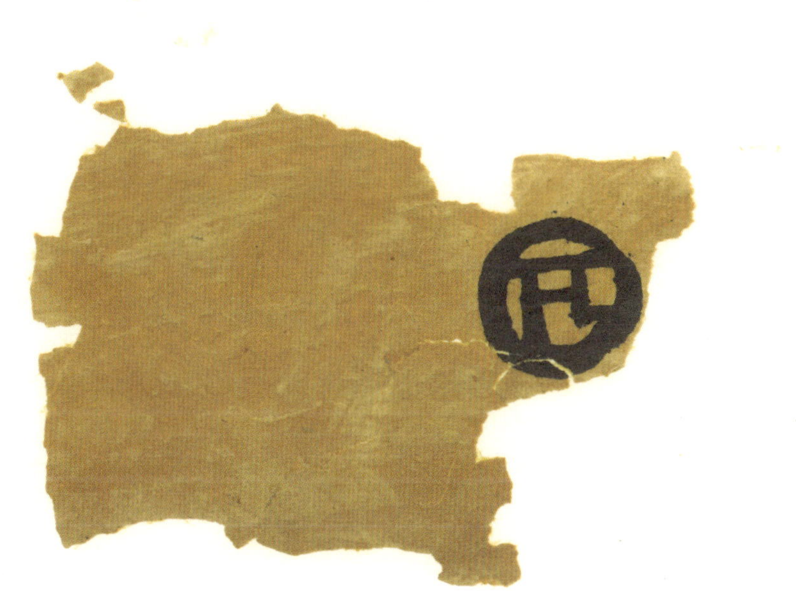

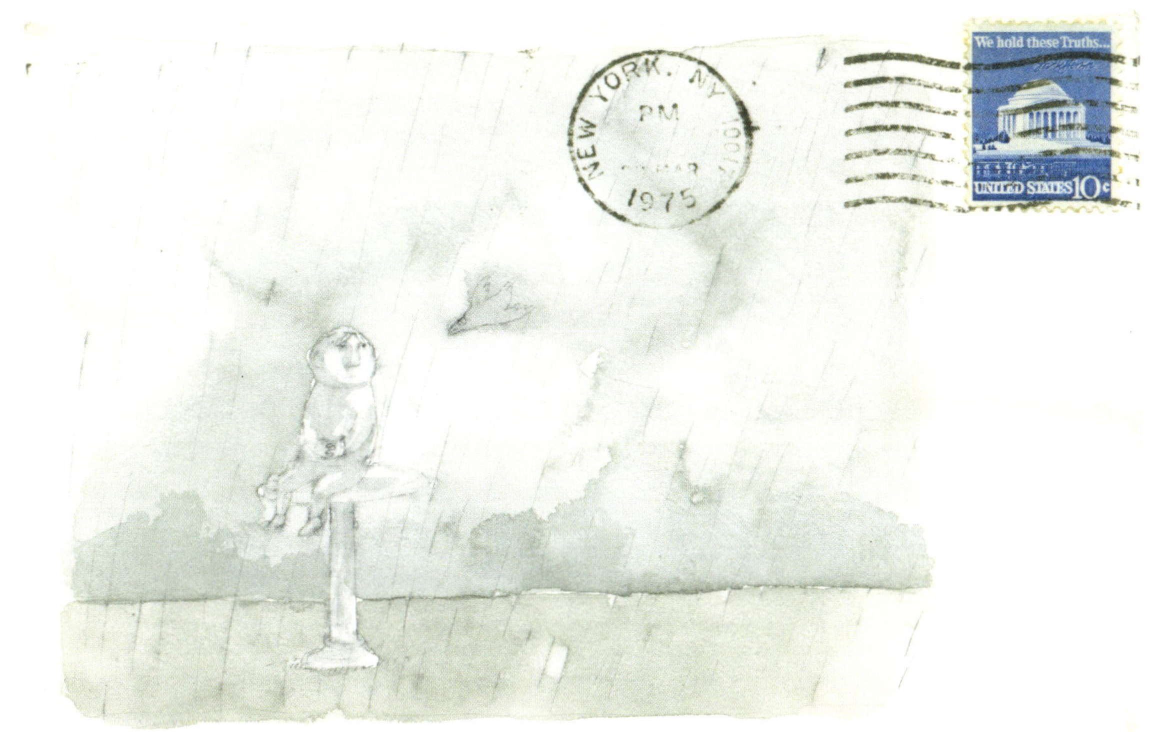

Tom Fitzharris, 76 Bank Street, New York, N.Y. 10014

XXXVIII

Thirty-Eight

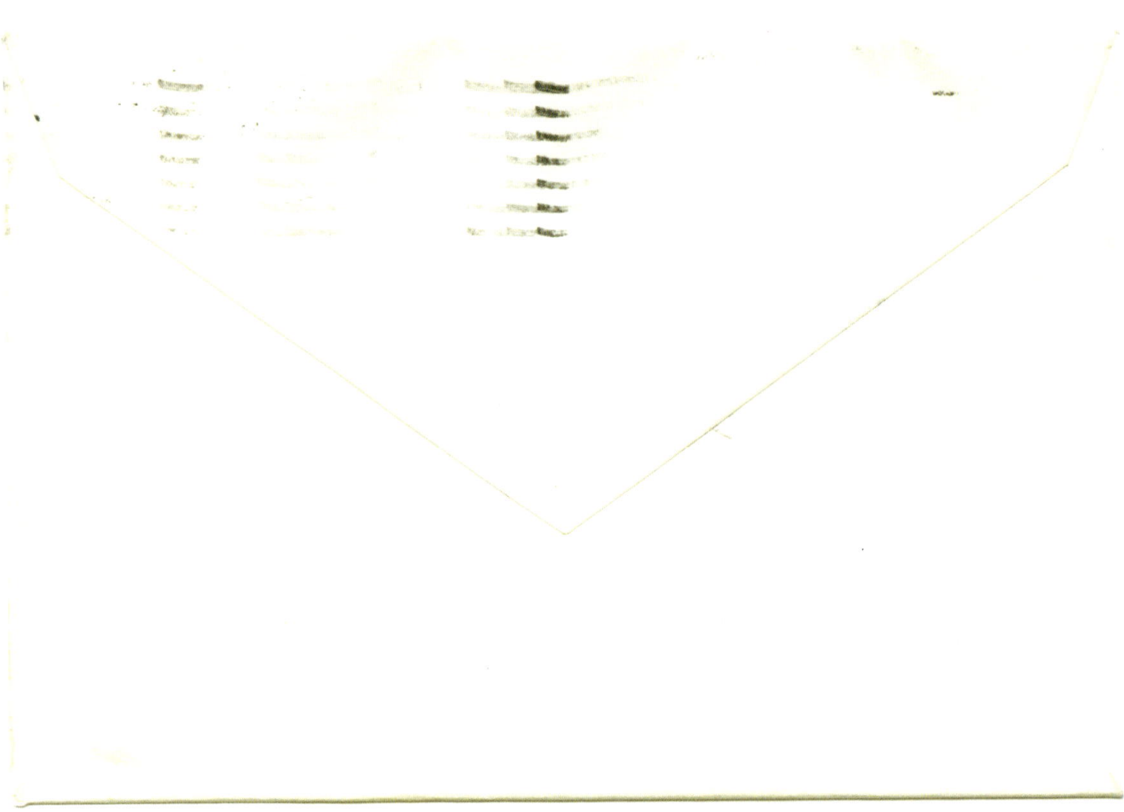

It rains across the country I remember.

MNEMOSYNE, *Trumbull Stickney*

Tom Fitzharris, 76 Bank Street, New York, N.Y. 10014
We hold these Truths...
UNITED STATES 10c
XXXIX

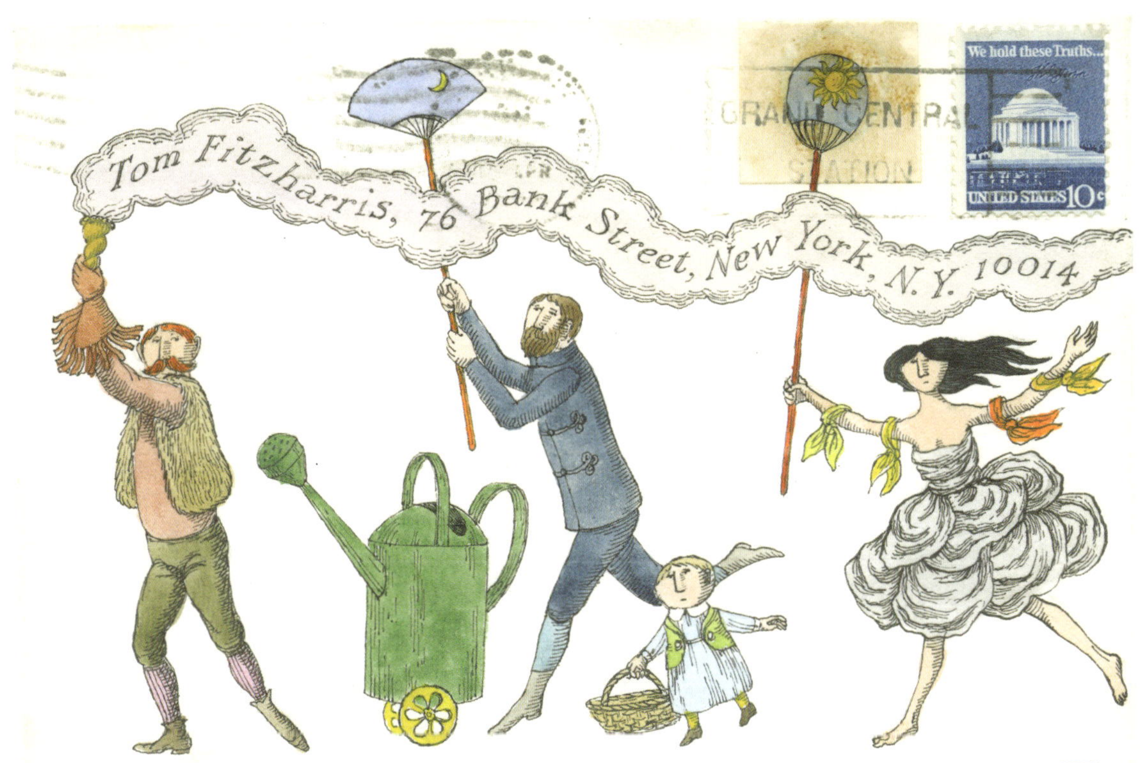

Thirty-Nine

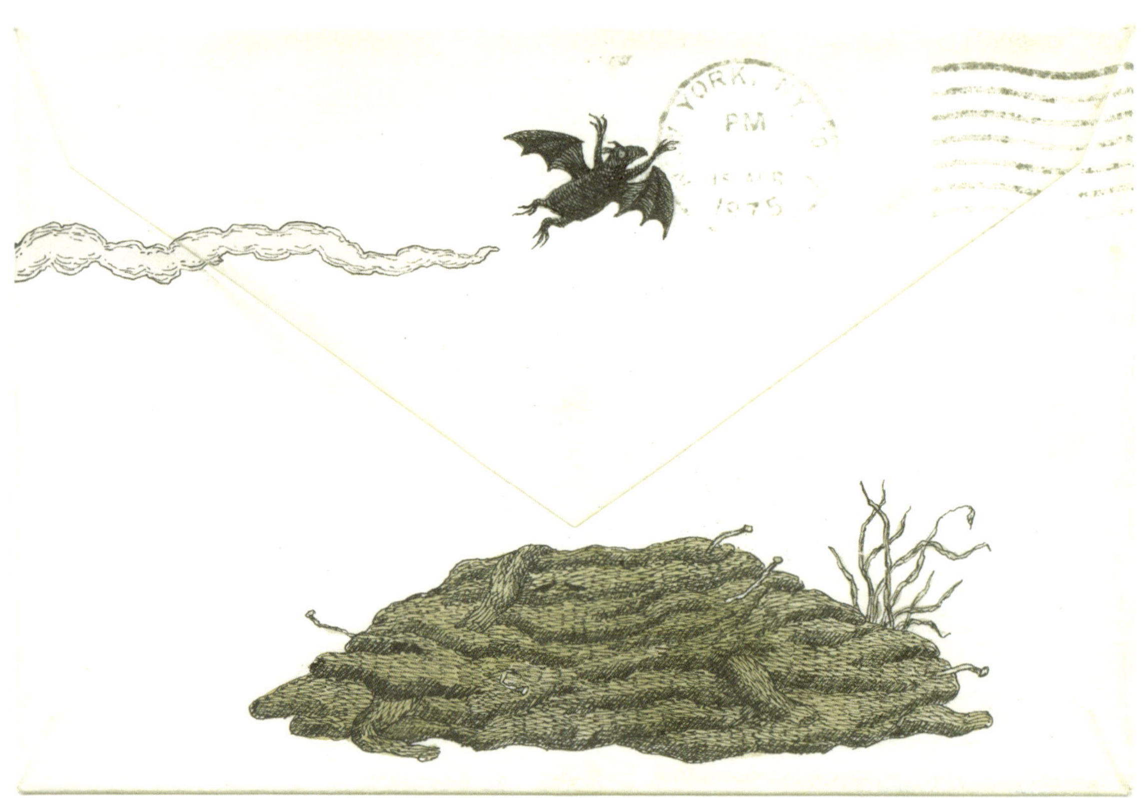
YORK,
PM

When you feel like that you often meet what you feel.

Ulysses

La Vie
L'Amour
Le Malheur
La Mort
L'Épinard
L'Art
Le Bon
L'OBSCURITÉ
TOM FITZHARRIS
76 BANK STREET
NEW YORK CITY 10014
AM
We hold these Truths...
UNITED STATES 10c

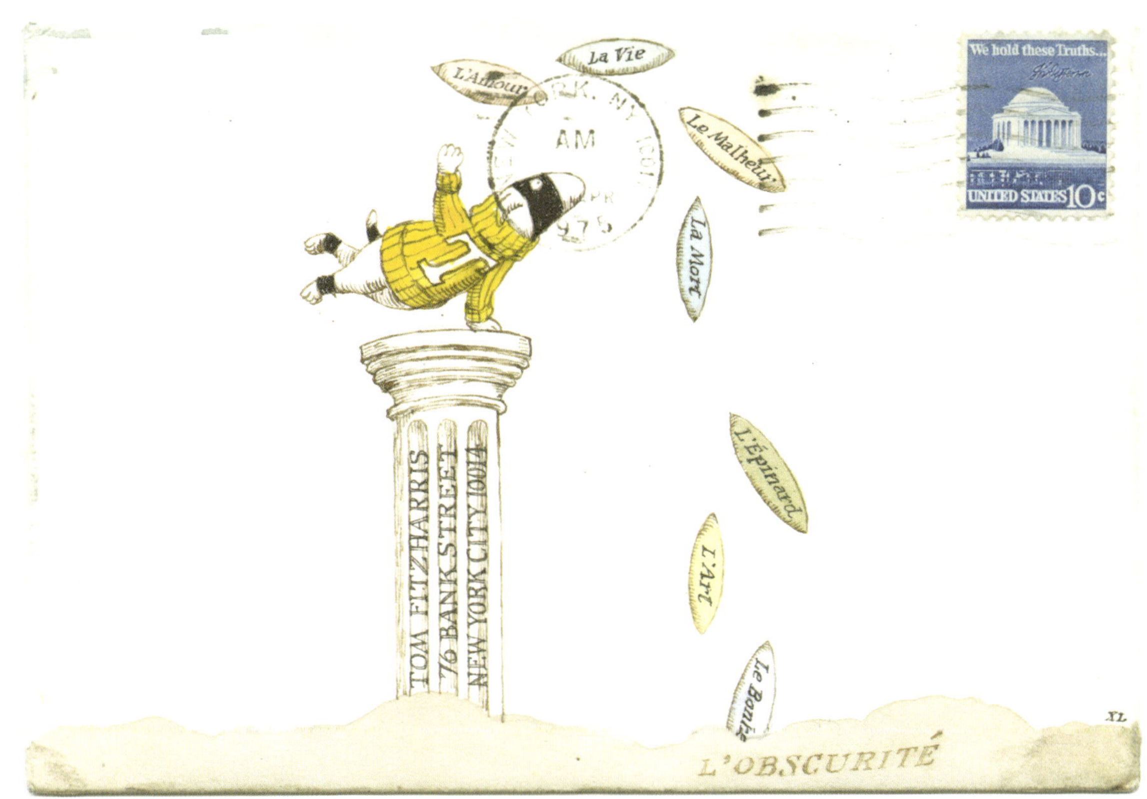

Forty

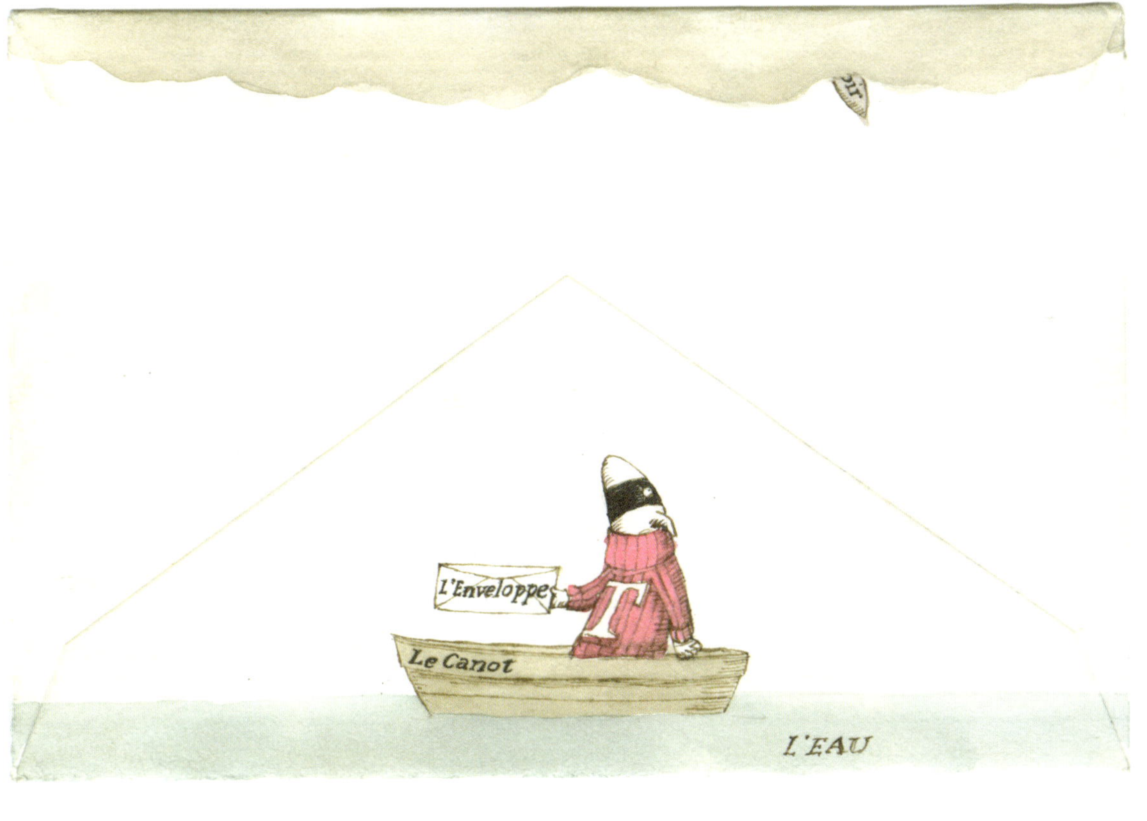
L'Enveloppe
Le Canot
L'EAU

It is difficult to retrace one's steps over paths which have been mistakenly chosen through being too clever.

Family Sayings, NATALIA GINZBURG

Please do not turn the page until the accompaniment is concluded.

Recital program

Forty-One

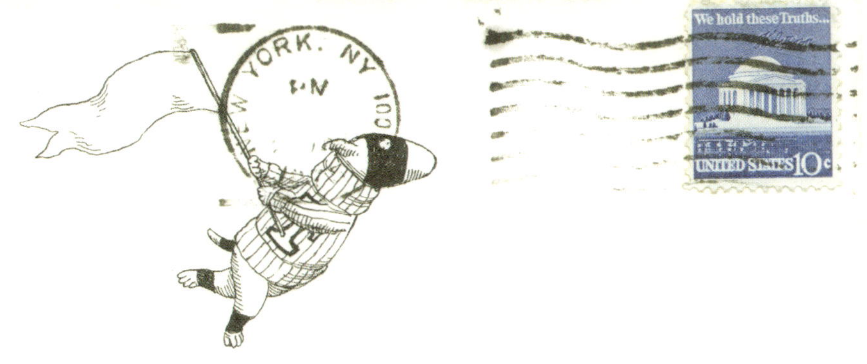

Tom FITZHARRIS,

76 BANK STREET,

NEW YORK, NEW YORK,

10014.

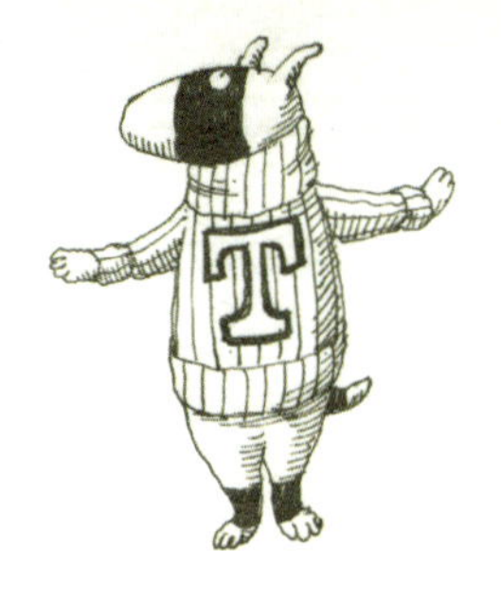

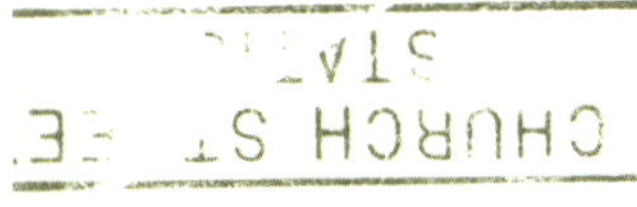
CHURCH ST
STA

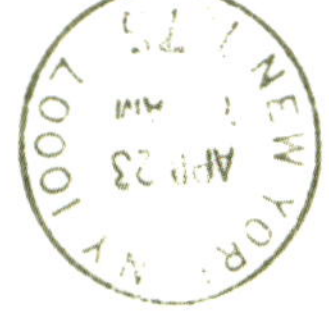
NEW YORK NY 10007
APR 23
AM

La paralysie est le commencement de la sagesse.

PICABIA (des oeufs)

SEND DOGEAR WRYDE POSTCARDS
NEW YORK, NY 10017
PM
APR
We hold these Truths...
UNITED STATES 10c
TOM Fitzharris,
76 BANK STREET,
NEW YORK, NEW YORK,
10014.
XLII

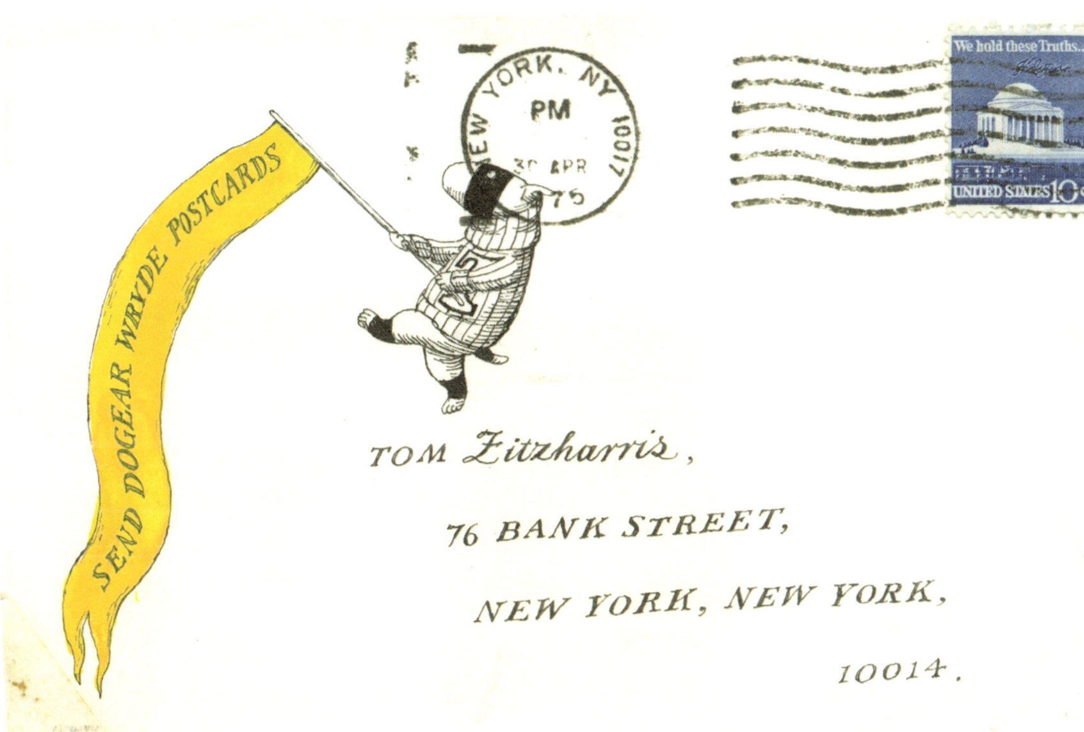

Forty-Two

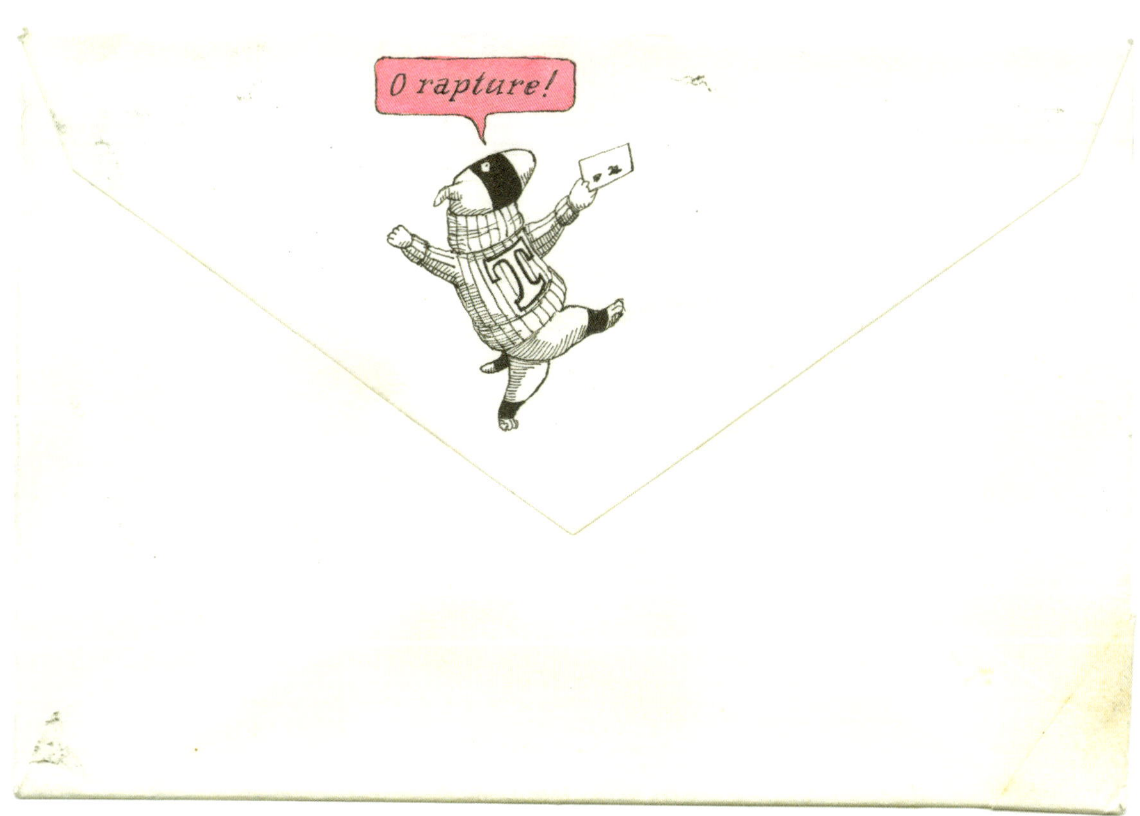
O rapture!
T

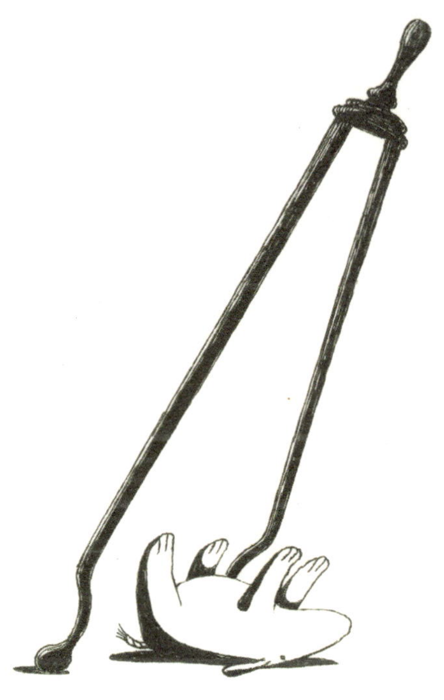

POSTCARD

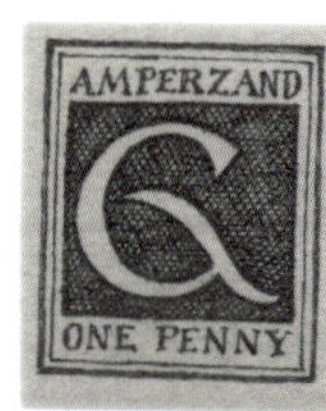

DOGEAR WRYDE POSTCARDS

Menaced Objects Series No. 8

Stuffed Toy Being Trifled With by Fire-Tongs

XLIII (copy)
BRIGHTEN
THE DAY
WITH
DOGEAR WRYDE
POSTCARDS
TOM FITZHARRIS
76 BANK STREET
NEW YORK CITY
10014

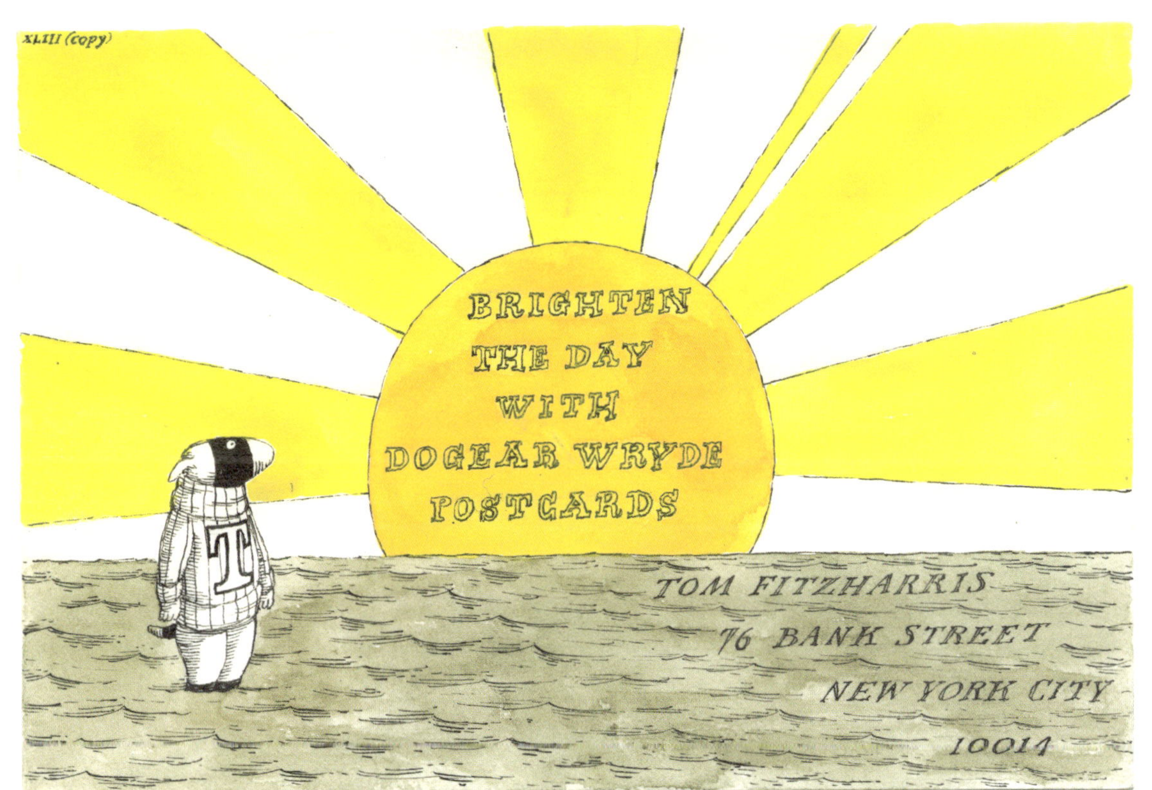

Forty-Three

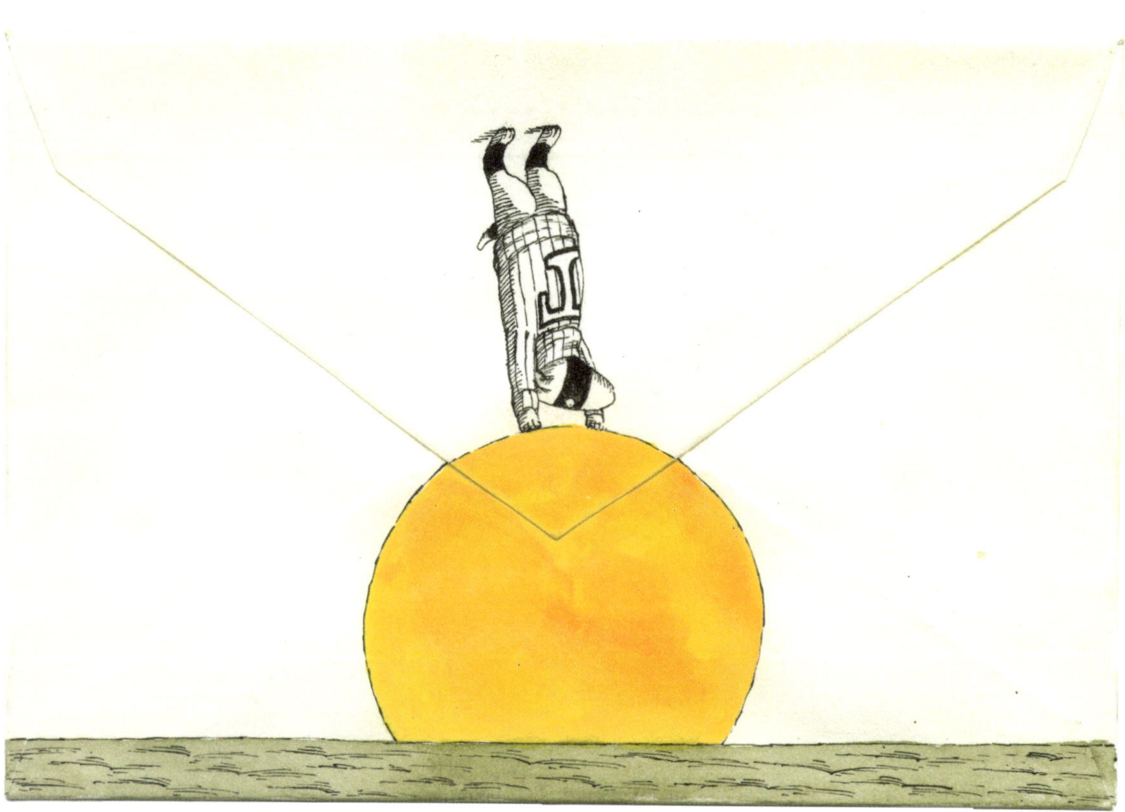

XLIV (copy)
DOGEAR WRYDE POSTCARDS
Tom Fitzharris, 76 Bank Street, New York, New York, 10014

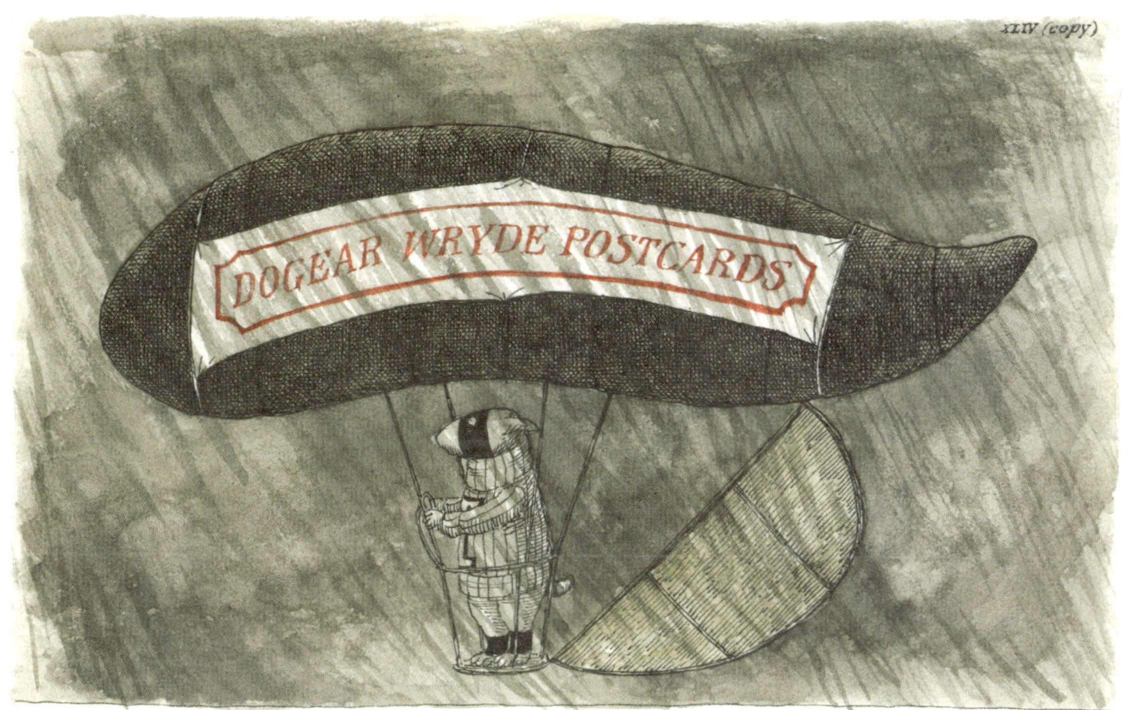

Forty-Four

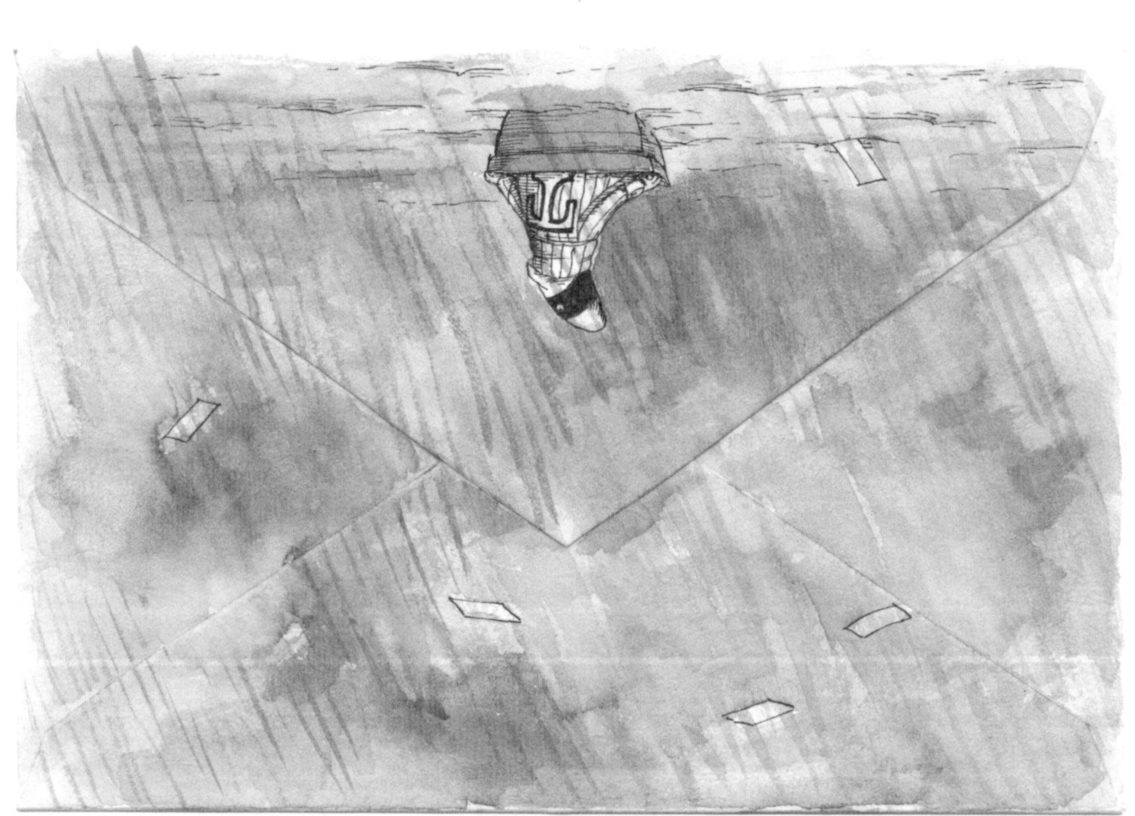

Tom Fitzharris,
76 Bank Street,
New York City,
10014.

XLV

Forty-Five

EDWARD GOREY

One may speculate pleasureably that the entire germ of *A la Recherche du Temps Perdu* might be contained in a sentence of Hardy's closely following the passage (from *A Pair of Blue Eyes*) quoted: "Time closed up like a fan before him."

Part of footnote, Brian Aldiss, *Billion Year Spree*

la nuit d'été
un timbre des Îles Maladroites
le feuillage
Proust
IV
le coussin
le divan
la fenêtre ouverte
L'hédonisme
des nocturnes de Chopin
We hold these Truths...
UNITED STATES 10c
le gramophone
la bière étrangère
les oreos froides
Tom Fitzharris, 76 Bank Street, New York, New York, 10014
XLVI

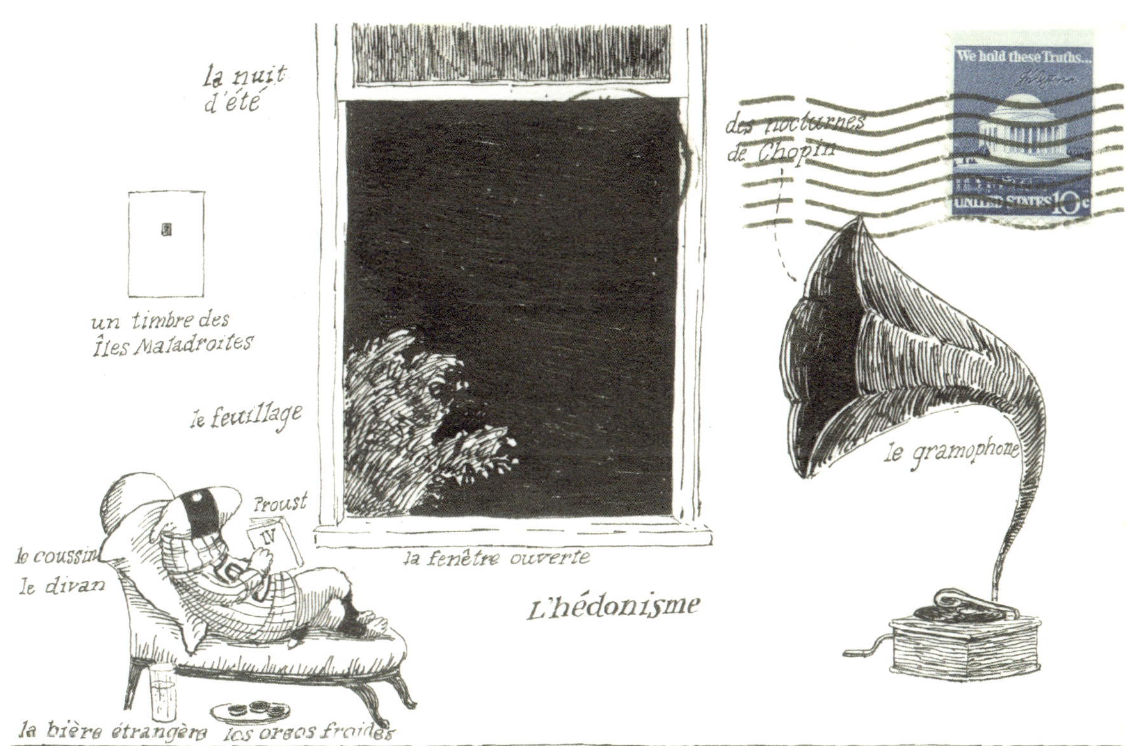

Forty-Six

EDWARD GOREY

To select for one's chamber a woodcut after Constable or Gainsborough is at all events to give proof of a capacity for civilisation.

The Nether World, GEORGE GISSING

timbré, -e p. adj. Stamped; (fam.) a bit cracked, dotty.

The Concise Oxford French Dictionary

We hold these Truths...
UNITED STATES 10c
Tom Fitzharris,
76 Bank Street,
New York City,
10014.
XLVII

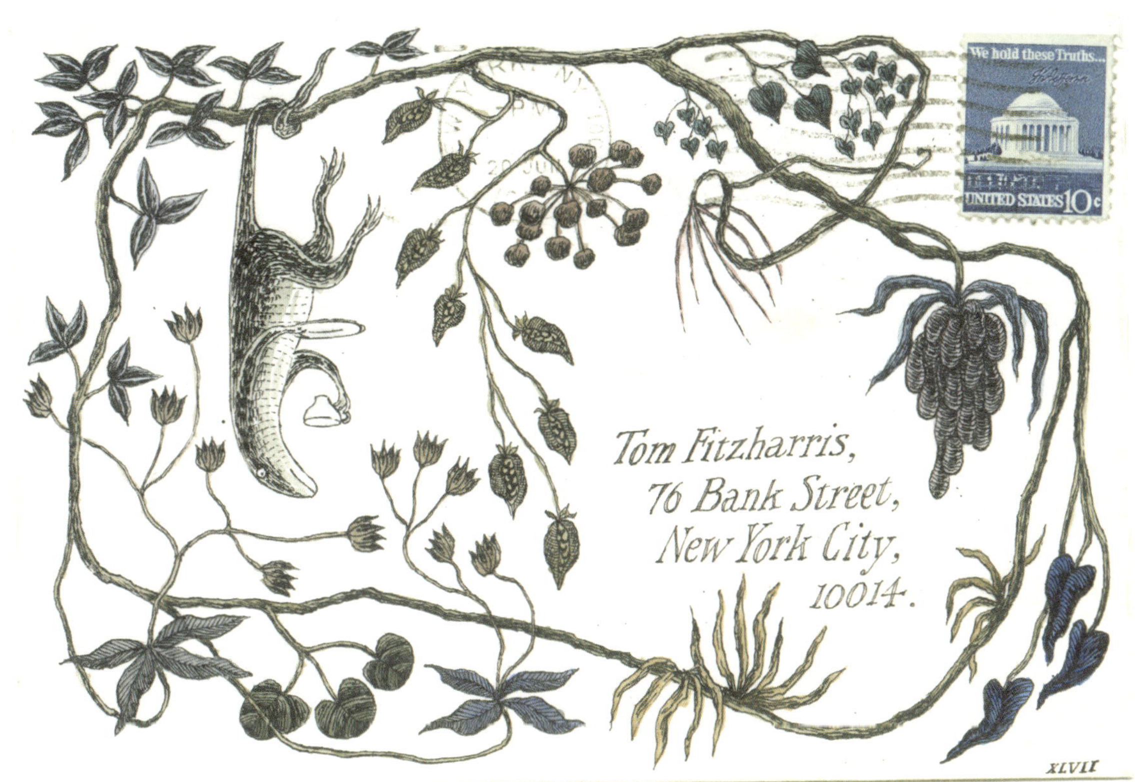

Forty-Seven

EDWARD GOREY

Is there such a thing in this world as speech that has but one simple interpretation, one for him who utters it and for him who hears?

The Nether World, GEORGE GISSING

E. Gorey,
Barnstable,
Mass, 02630
We hold these Truths...
UNITED STATES 10c
Tom Fitzharris,
76 Bank Street,
New York, N.Y. 10014
XLVIII

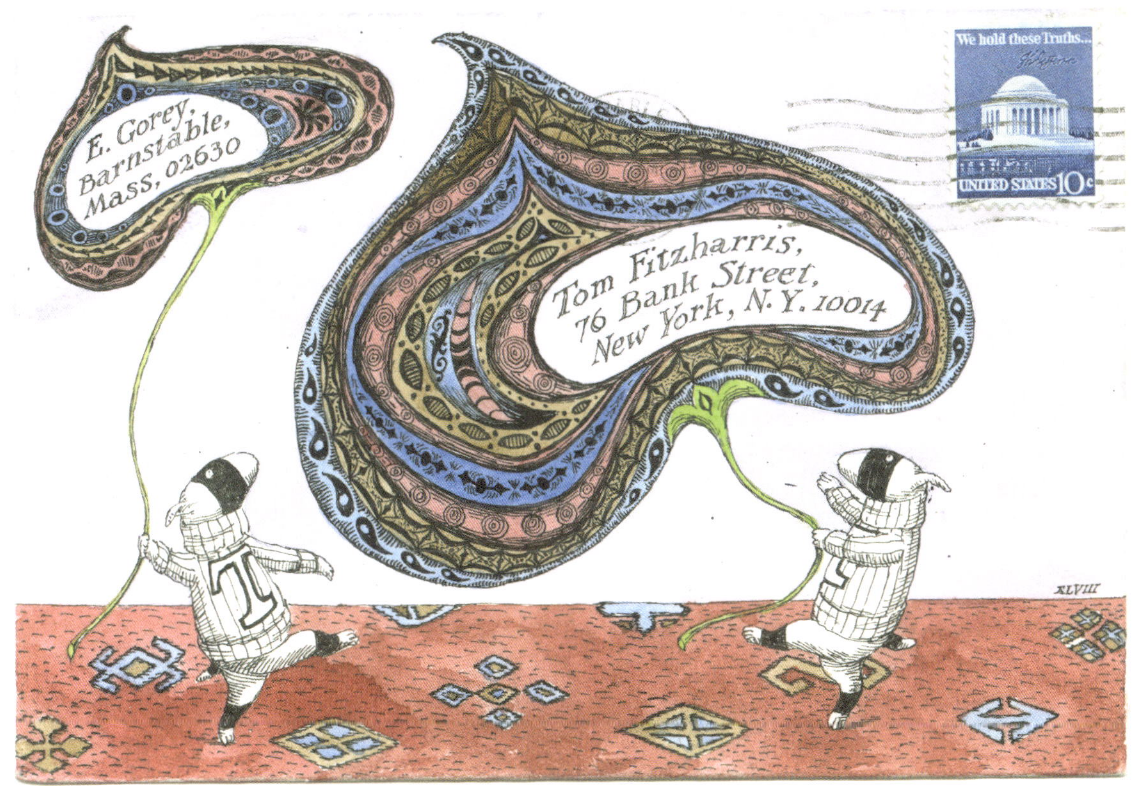

Forty-Eight

Life's all right if you can stand it.

Sandy Kimball, a schizophrenic, Edmund Wilson's favorite cousin, quoted in THE TWENTIES

XLIX
We hold these Truths...
UNITED STATES 10c
Tom Fitzharris,
76 Bank Street,
New York, N.Y.
10014
L'Enfant aux ficelles

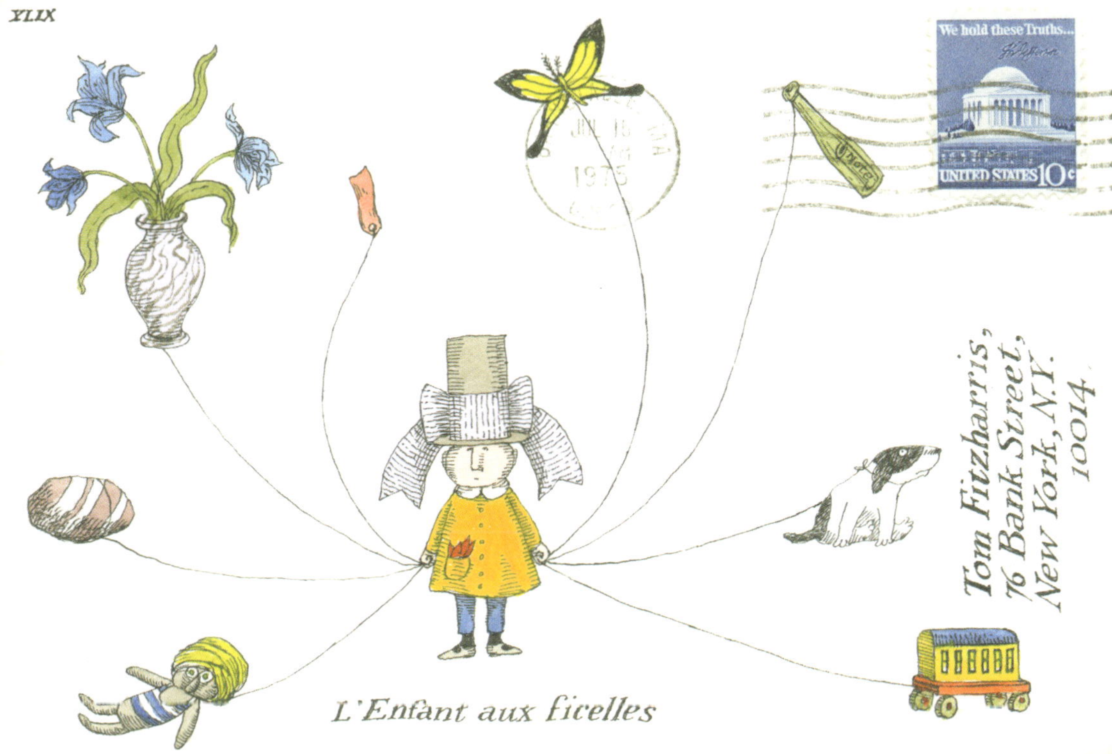

Forty-Nine

02630

I often think I am possessed with things I really want, but when I come to search find it only a shadow.

12 June ?1725, Diary of a Dutch sailor put ashore on the Island of Ascension (first published in the HARLEIAN MISCELLANY *of 1746)*

Tuesday morning, 15.vii.75

I trust you had an interesting time with Twyla et al, and that you got home before dawn.

I was supposed to go to Nantucket this morning to see the stage I'm designing the second act of Swan Lake for, but it was fogged in (Nantucket) so here I am.

The humidity is very boring, even here. It makes trying to be interested/interesting very difficult.

You are no doubt wondering what I will be like; so am I.

Fifty

We hold these Truths...
UNITED STATES 10c
We hold these Truths...
UNITED STATES 10c
Tom Fitzharris,
76 Bank Street,
New York, N.Y.
10014

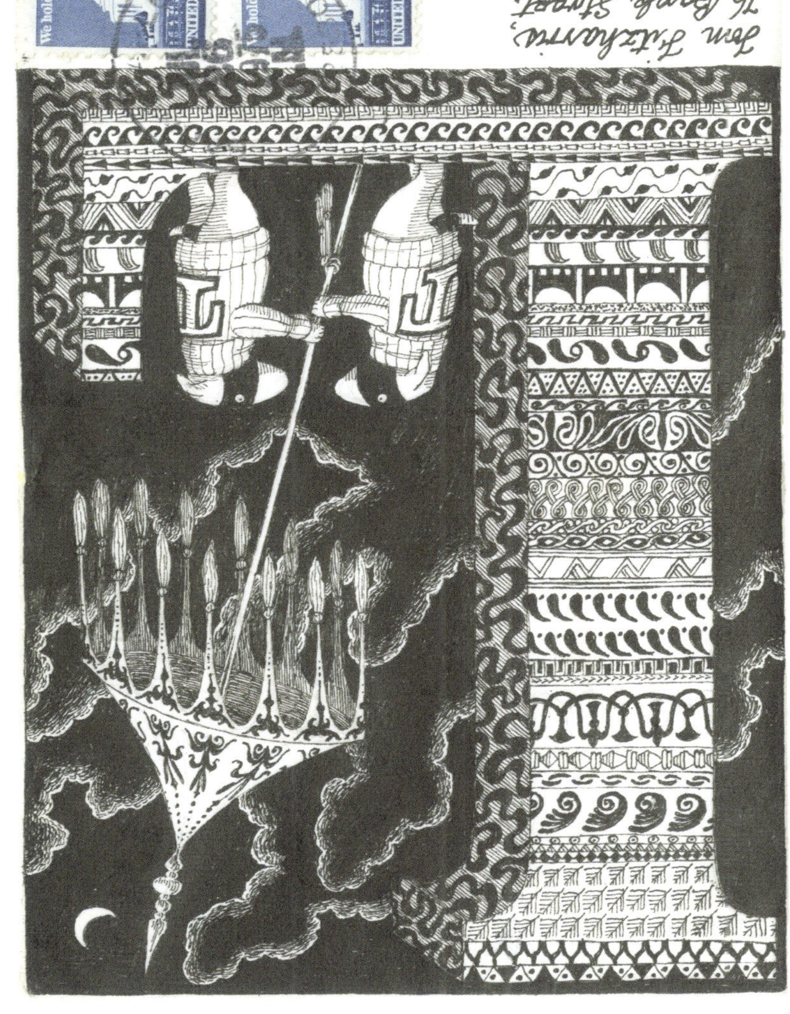

02630

What a resource it is under fatigue and irritation to have your drawing-room well supplied with small mats, which would always be ready if ever you wanted to set anything on them!

GEORGE ELIOT, *Scenes of Clerical Life*

Thursday afternoon

Where has the week gone?

They have just finished building us a new chimney on the marina side of the house so that the flue from the furnace can be removed from the fireplace in the livin room; in a rash moment I said I would pay for the whol proceeding. The price of bricks is ruinous.

I think I had all sorts of~~f~~ brief oddments on ~~the~~ my mind the last several days and now I can't seem to think of any of them. I do hope you get this letter before I turn up myself but it seems doubtful. The parasol and the L are still to be filled in.

The day is about to be filled with mysterious comings and goings, and I think I had better try and get some drawing done, even if my drawing paper resembles damp sponge to work on up here in the attic...

Notes

ONE The *T*'s on the dogs stand for "Ted and Tom." However, Ted was very much a cat person.

Wallace Stevens (1879–1955) was one of the great American poets of the twentieth century.

TWO The quote is by the poet Henri de Régnier (1864–1936) and translates to: "The delicious and ever new pleasure of a useless occupation." The composer Maurice Ravel (1875–1937) published his *Valses nobles et sentimentales* in a piano version in 1911 and an orchestral version in 1912.

THREE The inspiration for this envelope came from Ted seeing the Wushu (Martial Arts) Company perform in New York City in June 1974 as part of a US–China cultural exchange.

The quote by the painter Paul Gauguin (1848–1903) translates as: "Life is made from different chunks. With no links, like in dreams."

The note from Ted is handwritten, because the New York City Ballet was in Saratoga for the summer and he had driven up to see them, seemingly typewriter-less.

FOUR A typical Ted detail. On this fourth envelope, he doesn't use the usual Roman numeral "IV" it's an alternative version more often used in the Middle Ages, "IIII". This is the first numbered envelope.

Jorge Luis Borges (1899–1986) was an Argentinian poet, writer, and translator.

FIVE Anne Thackery Ritchie (1837–1919) was a Victorian writer and the eldest daughter of William Makepeace Thackeray.

SIX *Gorgias* is a Socratic dialogue written around 380 BC by the Greek philosopher Plato (ca. 427–348 BC).

On the "wobble": although he used the term often, Ted never did explain to me what he meant by it.

SEVEN The "crocodile in the sewers of Constantinople" that Ted was drawing was a part of a series "*Les Mystères de Constantinople*" which appeared in *The New York Review of Books* on and off throughout 1975.

Guillaume Apollinaire (1880–1918), French poet and writer who served in the French Army in World War I and was a major influence on the surrealist movement.

EIGHT Godfrey Fox Bradby (1863–1947) was a schoolmaster of the Rugby School in the United Kingdom, as well as a writer of prose, poems, and more.

The 1927 novel *Mr. Balcony* by Clifford Henry Benn Kitchin (1895–1967) is described in the 2009 reprint copy thus: "Bored with the London summer, [Mr. Balcony] fills his yacht with assorted socialites, chief among them the beautiful, restless Gloria Swing, and heads for the torrid coast of Africa, where fate, they discover, can certainly prove worse than death."

NINE Ted wrote "The quote is the inscription, apparently much defaced so that no one is even sure that's what the letters are, over the entrance to the Bomarzo Gadens. It means 'Every thought flies,' or 'Every thought flies away.'" The Bomarzo which is known for its grotesque sculptures scattered across a surreal landscape.

There were two places in the world that Ted had always wanted to visit. One was the Bomarzo, and the other was the Ryōan-ji Temple garden, a Zen rock garden in Kyoto.

Jean Cocteau, (1889–1963) French writer, poet, and filmmaker.

Marcel Proust (1871–1922) French writer best known for *In Search of Lost Time*.

TEN *L'heure bleue* or the "blue hour" is when the sun goes down and the sky is a deep blue, almost black. I introduced the term to Ted.

While he was sending these letters to me, Ted started working on and then published a book with the title *L'heure Bleu*.

The "Mrs. Regera Dowdy" he mentions is an anagram for "Edward Gorey."

Nathaniel Hawthorne (1804–1864) American novelist, author of *The Scarlet Letter.*

ELEVEN & TWELVE John Masefield (1878–1967) was a poet laureate of the United Kingdom and the author of *The Midnight Folk* (1927).

THIRTEEN John Cage (1912–1992) was a musician, writer, and music theorist.

FOURTEEN Ted wrote of this envelope: "I have not a real idea in my head for the envelope so what I suspect it is going to end up explained by is the fact that Gilbert (of & Sullivan) had a similar set of blocks—male members of the cast were 3" high, females 2½" and different colours denoted different voices–and with them he plotted out the details of his stage production in advance."

The Kokinshū was an early tenth century anthology of Japanese poetry.

FIFTEEN The blue slip is a nineteenth century pew ticket. You received one when you paid for your family's spots in church. Ted never told me where he found it.

Ted wrote about the postcards he included: "I think you will find the enclosed postcards (which I could not bring myself to send unenveloped through the mail) more something (I doubt if the word is 'meaningful') if you regard them as being a triptych. But then again."

Burt Britton was in charge of the review copies at the Strand Bookstore.

Arnold Bennett (1867–1931) English writer, known for the novel *Old Wives' Tale*.

SIXTEEN Ted wrote this about the note card: "Sandy Wason (probably) was an eccentric English clergyman who wrote (hopelessly unattainable) light verse, a novel called, if I recollect, *Palefox*, about which all I know is that it is always snowing in it (v. *The Unstrung Harp*), and the only book I have of his, an anthology of prefaces and introductions he compiled with someone else."

SEVENTEEN R. H. Grenville was the pseudonym of the British Canadian poet Beatrice Rowley (1917–2017).

EIGHTEEN Ted on the envelope art: "All the blue bottles are a recollection of a window full of them in one of the antique shops I stopped in after you left that Sunday. The sun coming through them is not reproducible, at least by me."

The Duchess of Malfi is a Jacobean-era play written by John Webster (1578–1632) and first performed in 1613 or 1614.

NINETEEN Ted, on the envelope: "The explanation, or lack of it, for the envelope is that when I was driving Sandwichwards on 6A one day this week I saw an oar somewhat the colour of these floating in the air as it were, though actually it was nailed at either end to two uprights of a porch."

Ted on the note card: "The quote in with this is from Heaven only knows where or what, and is meant to have no significance apart from its beauty."

TWENTY Of the first quote, Ted wrote, "Author of *A Visit to the Sea-Side* unknown; it's an anonymous 19th century children's book I have lying around somewhere."

Ted wrote: "I now have a blackbound sketch book in which I have orderly entered what I can remember about previous envelopes, quotes, etc. There are a few gaps. Anyway." This is what he used to redraw envelopes forty-three and forty-four.

Albert Camus (1913–1960) French writer, philosopher, journalist, and political activist. Author of *The Stranger*, and winner of the 1957 Nobel Prize in Literature.

TWENTY-ONE Ted wrote of the winged dogs on the front: "The wings of the dogs were vaguely suggested by dragonflies' wings, translated from the nature in my own pawky way. (I never had any books of good quality.)"

Urabe Kenkō was a 14th century Buddhist monk and author of *Tsurezuregusa*.

TWENTY-TWO In his notes on this envelopes, Ted describes the objects the dogs are standing on as "mauve iced oatmeal cakes."

Ivy Compton-Burnett (1884–1969) was an English novelist.

TWENTY-THREE Ted wrote in his notes for this envelope: "Chartreuse to orange Loie Fuller drapes." Fuller (1862–1928) was an American dancer and lighting designer. Amiel on the first notecard is Henri Frédéric Fredric Amiel, (1820–1880), a Swiss moral philosopher.

Carl Jung (1875–1961) was a Swiss psychiatrist and psychotherapist who founded the school of analytical psychology.

TWENTY-FOUR *Bussy D'Ambois* was written by George Chapman (ca. 1559–1634) in the late sixteenth century. Ted: "Do you think the enclosed quote means anything, and if so, what? Or do you suppose I copied it down wrong in the long, long ago?"

TWENTY-FIVE Heraclitus (a. 540–480 BC) was a pre-Socratic ancient Greek philosopher.

TWENTY-SIX The red leaf on the back of the envelope is the same color as the leaf I'd picked up as Ted and I hiked down the Flume Gorge in the White Mountains in New Hampshire on Saturday, October 19, 1974.

TWENTY-SEVEN I suspect the two characters on the envelope are from the 1968 Cuban film *Lucía*. In the movie, there was a marvelous enormous 1895 dining room whose walls were hung with hundreds of plates.

The critic Hugh Kenner translated this line from Keats for his book *The Pound Era* which Ted was reading at the time.

TWENTY-EIGHT The front of the envelope is a reference to one of the limericks Ted included in this letter.

The quote translates to: "Always tripe."

TWENTY-NINE I don't remember what the "incident" was, but it did not teach me that.

THIRTY Ted helped me paint the kitchen in my first apartment. The buckets of white paint on the envelope ("A Wrong Shade," "Another Wrong Shade," "Yet Another Wrong Shade") refer to how I had trouble deciding what shade of white to select. I used to joke that I owned the only large-scale oil painting Ted ever made.

Wyndham Lewis (1882–1957) was a British painter and writer.

THIRTY-ONE The yellow "kitchen" and pink "bathroom" are reminders of the colors of those rooms in my apartment when I first moved in.

From *The New York Times*'s Dcember 29, 1974 review of *The End of Intelligent Writing* Ted quotes on the note card: "*The End of Intelligent Writing* isn't about that, and isn't itself as intelligently written as it could and should have been."

THIRTY-TWO This is the one envelope on which I thought the postmark was perfectly placed.

"Blutig" is a pun on Ted's last name in German.

THIRTY-FOUR I'd joked that I was adept at picking out interesting stones when Ted and I were at some ocean beach.

Louis-Ferdinand Céline (1894–1961) was a French novelist.

THIRTY-FIVE The French translates to "A foretaste of a future work" from a series titled *The Horrible Tassels.*

René Magritte (1898–1967) was a Belgian surrealist artist.

THIRTY-SIX Francis Bacon (1909–1992) was an Irish British painter.

THIRTY-SEVEN The envelope depicts depicts the heroine of Ted's enigmatic work *The Worsted Monster* in three costumes.

The quote translates to: "It was there, in particular, that I confirmed the truth that love, which we cry up as the source of our pleasures, is nothing more than an excuse for them."

Ted called the bat drawings "bat putti." "*Putti*" in Italian "small cupids"—so, "bat cupids."

The symbol glued to a note card is a Toulouse-Lautrec logo from a poster. It seems to be real. Ted sent it without explanation.

THIRTY-EIGHT Trumbull Stickney (1874–1904) was an American poet.

THIRTY-NINE The characters on the envelope are from Ted's *The Worsted Monster*, which he worked on starting in the 1950s but never completed. On the back is the titular Worsted monster.

The quote is from the novel *Ulysses* by the Irish novelist James Joyce (1882–1941).

FORTY Translations of the terms on the front of the envelope, top to bottom:

L'Amour: Love
La Vie: Life
L Malheur: Misfortune
La Mort: Death
L'Épinard: Spinach
L'Art: Art
Le Bonhe[ur]: Happiness
L'Obscurité: Obscurity

Back of envelope, top to bottom:

L'Eau: Water
Le Canot: The Canoe
L'Enveloppe: Envelope
[Le Bonhe]ur: Happiness

Natalia Ginzburg (1916–1991) was an Italian novelist and essayist.

FORTY-ONE Note card translation: "Paralysis is the first stage of wisdom."

Francis Picabia (1879–1953) was a French artist.

FORTY-TWO The name "Dogear Wryde" on the flag is another anagram for "Edward Gorey."

Ted and I had gone to postcard club meetings and bought postcards at shops, and then Ted started making his own.

FORTY-THREE & FORTY-FOUR These were the pair of envelopes that got lost in the mail and Ted then redrew, using the sketches in his notebook.

FORTY-FIVE The stamp drawing was inspired by the artist Donald Evans. Evans (1945–1977) painted watercolor postage stamps from imaginary countries—beautiful little pieces mounted as if they were being displayed in a stamp museum. Ted loved them and owned a few. His version is from a country he named Napoo.

Brian Aldiss (1925–2017) was a British science fiction writer.

FORTY-SIX This is the most personal envelope Ted sent me. It was of my new apartment, filled with some of my favorite things. A list of the translations:

L'hédonisme: Hedonism
la nuit d'été: summer night
un timbre des Île Maladroites: a postage stamp from the Clumsy Islands [an imaginary country, like Donald Evans work]
le feuillage: foliage
le coussin: the cushion
le divan: the sofa
la bière étrangère: imported beer
les oreos froides: frozen Oreo cookies
la fenêtre ouverte: open window
des nocturnes de Chopin: Chopin's Nocturnes
le gramophone: the gramophone

On *les oreos froides*: I was in the army stationed in Belgium, living off-post and having to cook for myself. Someone told me, "If you put Oreos in the fridge, it kills the sweetness." I told Ted about this and he loved it. Then he told the choreographer Jerome Robbins about it, who immediately replied, "Ted, everyone knows that."

FORTY-SEVEN George Gissing was an English novelist (1857–1903).

FORTY-NINE Translation: "Child with Strings."

Ted wrote of this envelope: "No explanation for the objects, through a small series of such drawings flits vaguely through my head, with different sets of objects so to speak attached in different ways to different people, things, etc."

FIFTY George Eliot, author of *Middlemarch*, was the pseudonym of Mary Ann Evans (1819–1880).

Acknowledgments

Andreas Brown
Former owner of The Gotham Book Mart; Ted's good friend and publisher of many of his books. Andreas originally approached me about doing this book.

Robert Greskovic
Writer, dance critic and Ted's close friend who answered and asked numerous important questions about Ted's life and art.

Christine von der Linn
Honey & Wax Booksellers. Her intimate knowledge of Ted's work and examination of each envelope, brought things to mind I hadn't remembered or considered.

Jed Perl
Who arranged for me to connect with New York Review Books for this project, and was a source of encouragement throughout the process.

Lucas Adams
Senior Editor, New York Review Books. His energy, design ideas and cultural knowledge were crucial in creating this book.

Anika Banister
Editorial Assistant, New York Review Books. She contributed in myriad ways on the production side—including gently reminding me of things I sometimes forgot.

About the Authors

Edward Gorey (1925–2000) was born in Chicago. He studied briefly at the Art Institute of Chicago, spent three years in the army as a clerk at a site that specialized in the testing of poison gas, and attended Harvard College, where he majored in French literature and roomed with the poet Frank O'Hara. In 1953 Gorey published *The Unstrung Harp*, the first of his many books, which include *The Curious Sofa*, *The Haunted Tea-Cosy*, and *The Epiplectic Bicycle*.

In addition to illustrating his own stories, Gorey provided drawings to many books for both children and adults. Of these, New York Review Books has published *The Haunted Looking Glass*, a collection of Gorey's favorite ghost stories; *The War of the Worlds* by H. G. Wells; *Men and Gods* by Rex Warner; and *Three Ladies Beside the Sea* and *He Was There from the Day We Moved In* by Rhoda Levine.

Tom Fitzharris was a close friend of Edward Gorey in the 1970s. He currently lives in New York City and gives tours at the Metropolitan Museum of Art.